What readers are saying about Cyndy's true story

"You don't so much read *The Dead Inside* as you watch, through a dark and hazy window, as a child's soul is destroyed. There's nothing you can do but cheer for her silently and hope she survives. Abused by her stepfather then betrayed by her own mother, Etler describes sixteen months of physical and mental torture in a government-endorsed facility that knew just how to skirt the system and avoid detection. Even more painful? The girl in these pages didn't need the so-called help Straight had to offer. All she needed was for society to do its job protecting children. A must-read for parents, teachers, counselors, and students."

—Mercy Pilkington, 2010 National Juvenile Detention Association Teacher of the Year

"Prepare yourself. On page one, a young Etler takes your hand, and she doesn't let go. This naïve girl, struggling to deal with a harsh home life, is sent to a drug rehabilitation center, a place where she has no business. Though condemned to sixteen months of darkness—figurative and literal—Etler shines a light on the controversial treatment of 'problem children.' You won't be able to put [this book] down, and you sure as hell won't root this hard for anyone else ever again."

—Rosella Eleanor LaFevre, Editor-in-Chief, *M.L.T.S. Magazine*

"We, the survivors of Straight, wish we could make you understand what it was like. That we could put you in our skin, take you back in time, and sit you down in group. So you could motivate all day. And hear the screams. And feel the loss of yourself. We want to convey the self-betrayal, the omnipotent, alien reality of Straight, Inc. In [her memoir], Etler honors the many of us who still can't talk about it, and the many that were unable to survive. Somehow, Etler tells her story without making it about her."

—Marcus Chatfield, author of *Institutionalized Persuasion: The Technology of Reformation in Straight, Incorporated and the Residential Teen Treatment Industry*

THE DEAD INSIDE

A TRUE STORY

cyndy etler

Cover design by Connie Gabbert
Cover image © Nina Masic/Trevillion Images
Internal image © ISMODE/Thinkstock

This book is a memoir. It reflects the author's present recollections of experiences over a period of time. Some names and characteristics have been changed, some events have been compressed, and some dialogue has been re-created.

Published by Sourcebooks Fire, an imprint of Sourcebooks, Inc.
P.O. Box 4410, Naperville, Illinois 60567-4410
(630) 961-3900
Fax: (630) 961-2168
www.sourcebooks.com

Originally published as *Straightling: A Memoir* in 2012 in the United States by CreateSpace Independent Publishing Platform.

Library of Congress Cataloging-in-Publication data is on file with the publisher.

Printed and bound in the United States of America.
WOZ 10 9 8 7 6 5 4 3 2 1

For all you "troubled teens,"
who would totally stop being "trouble"
if someone would just be nice to you.

NOTE TO READER

You're not going to believe this. Seriously, nobody does. But this stuff happened, right here in America. In the warehouse down the street.

The warehouse had a name: Straight, Incorporated. Straight called itself a drug rehab for kids, but most of us had barely even smoked weed. Take me, for example. In September, at age thirteen, I smoked it for the first time. I tried it smoking again in October. In November, I got locked up in Straight—for sixteen months. The second we entered the building, we all stopped being kids. We stopped being humans. Instead, we were Straightlings.

Other than my father and me, each person you read about here has a fake name. Many of the Straightlings are smooshed-together versions of different people, but everything happened exactly how I describe it. If you want proof, hit the epilogue. There you'll find court records, canceled checks, newspaper reportage, and Straight, Inc. internal documents. Want more proof? Go online and read all of the survivor stories that are just like mine.

And to my fellow Straightlings? Put your armor on. You're going back on front row.

SIGN IN AND SIGN OUT

I never was a badass. Or a slut, a junkie, or a stoner like they told me I was. I was just a kid looking for something good, something that felt like love. I was a wannabe in a Levi's jean jacket. Anybody could see that. Except my mother. And the staff at Straight.

So maybe I didn't find a substitute family. Maybe I didn't find love. I found other stuff instead. Pink Floyd, for example. And God, and Marlboro Reds. And Bridgeport, this city where it's always dark, even at noon on Sundays. Only problem was, those were the exact things Straight used to prove you were an addict. You know: listening to druggie music, trying "gateway" drugs, running away from home…and then, before I could even learn how to smoke pot right, my mother trapped me in this warehouse full of teen savages. Straight, Inc.

From the outside, Straight was a drug rehab. But on the inside, it was…well, it was something else.

1

REPORT ANY SUSPICIOUS-LOOKING CHARACTER ON GROUNDS

The problem with me is that I never have the right pants. Think about it. When you go to the city, all you see are girls swiveling their hips, trying to make you notice the name on their butt. And it's not just in the city. When I lived in Stamford, the recess yard at my elementary school was this cornucopia of designer jeans. All the girls had at least one pair from the good brands, and some girls had all four Jordache pocket styles.

Designer-jean girls are always named, like, Heather or Samantha or Jessica. They wear their richness all casual, like a perfume. I spent every recess on the sidelines—watching them, trying to learn popularity—while wearing my big sister Kim's hand-me-down corduroys. I had three pairs, in a rainbow of depressing colors: beige, evergreen, and maroon. This one time, the three most popular girls in the whole sixth grade crossed the blacktop to get to me. I was all, *Oh my God! Is this really happening?* You can guess how *that* went.

Popular Girl:	What brand are those jeans, Cyndy?
Me:	These? These are a new kind of designer jeans—Garan. I have two Jordache and three Sasson at home, but I can't wear them to school. Only on weekends, when I visit my boyfriend in Norwalk.

I was like, *Yeah! Now they'll really like me—I have designer jeans* and *a boyfriend!* Here's what she said back.

Popular Girl:	Well, you call them Garan, but I call them Garanimals.

Oh my God. Garanimals is Sears-brand kids clothes, and Garan is totally the preteen version. She saw through my lie, and made me pay for it in front of everyone. What's that disease where everybody stays away from you 'cause, like, your limbs are falling off? Oh yeah, leprosy. I'm a poor-kid leper in a rich girl's world.

Once we moved out to Podunk Monroe though, the pants thing got easier. People in Monroe worship Levi's, not designer jeans. And Levi's have only one pocket design. So it's a lot easier to keep up. Plus, since moving to Monroe—this is the really good thing—I get to steal my sister Kim's best clothes since she's never here.

Losing her stuff is just the price Kim pays for being so lucky. Seriously. How does she get to stay with some church family in Stamford for her senior year while my mother and step-thing Jacque move us to this hick town? Friday nights, I'm looking for a hiding place where Jacque and his itchy hands won't find me while Kim walks around the Stamford mall, having guys whistle at her. I swear. If I didn't need Him as a friend so bad, this could make me wonder if God's even out there.

But actually, the friend thing has gotten better since I moved to Monroe. And it's pretty much because of my pants. Well, Kim's pants. When Kim does everyone a favor and visits Monroe, she switches the clothes she'll bring back to Stamford. That's how I get her good stuff. Last time she left behind the most awesome Levi's ever. 501s! Button fly! And they fit me! So now, because I have 501s, I'm cool. And because I'm cool, I got my best friend. Joanna.

Joanna's from Bridgeport, which is the murder capital of the United States. But her parents bought a second house in Monroe because *Oh, it's safe! And so pretty!* Really, though? They bought a house here because it's, like, one hundred percent white. Their Bridgeport house is right on the edge of Father Panik Village, which is where bad Masuk High boys go to buy drugs from black guys. And it really is a shady place, I guess. Joanna found a loaded gun in her backyard bushes. She thinks if she hadn't showed it to her father, she'd still be living there. But now, instead, she lives in Monroe. Too bad for her, but lucky for me.

Joanna's told me all about Bridgeport. In detail. When I picture it, I get this feeling like there's a mountain of shattered glass in front of me, and I can reach out and touch it. It's glittery and scary, and anything can happen there. And we're going tonight and staying for the whole weekend!

So of course I'm wearing my 501s, plus my denim jacket. I've gotta wear my Keds since I have no other shoes, but here's what's good: I get to finally wear those Barbie-pink undies I found hidden in Kim's dresser. You don't even pull them on; you have to *tie* them on, with little ribbons on the sides! I've been saving them for a special dress-up occasion, but if tonight's not special, I don't know what is.

Joanna's dad, Mr. Azore, looks like Mario from *Donkey Kong*. He's short and wide, and he has that kind of mustache that curls at the ends. I really like him, because he laughs a lot. And whenever Joanna says, "Dad, I'm going out tonight. Can I have some money?" he hands her a twenty. A *twenty*.

Other than their laugh, Joanna is more like her mother. They're built like the ladders Mario has to climb: tall and rectangular, with nothing extra up top. Listen, I friggin' love Joanna, but she's got bad eyeliner and guy hair. Sorry, Jo.

The ride to the Azores' Bridgeport house is better than *anything*. It's like freedom, like me and Jo are the dudes in a motorcycle movie. My window's rolled all the way down, and Mr. and Mrs. Azore are so cool, they don't make me roll it up when we get on the highway. I flip between asking Jo what we'll do tonight—"Hang out. Go see what the guys are doing."—and staring out the window, trying not to ask for more stories about "the guys."

The changes in scenery remind me of kids' book pictures, how they tell the story better than the words do. Outside the window in Monroe, it's all boring, clean streets and fresh grass. But the longer we're on the highway, the tighter and darker everything gets. Halfway to Bridgeport, in Trumbull, there are still trees, but the slabs of rock on either side of the road are all graffitied out.

Then you hit Bridgeport and *bang!* It's like someone pulled down a screen. Everything's suddenly gray. By the time you're off the exit and going by the gas station, there's nothing natural at all, just hunks of cars stripped down to shells and rocky dirt lots. But somehow you can tell, in the middle of all the deadness, this place is where *real* life happens.

So, like, life is pretty much perfect here. Joanna takes me out behind their house and shows me where she found the gun, and then we order pizza like it's no big. By eight o'clock we're out walking, four fives in Jo's pocket and a curfew of "Not too late, girls." Dag.

Joanna takes me by the houses of her Bridgeport friends, Mary and Torpedo Tits. And um…is it possible she wants to keep me all to herself? Because she didn't even tell them we were coming. We have to sneak up and then run right past their houses. I'm trying really hard to be cool, but I can't stop my hyena laugh, even when Joanna cups her hand around my mouth and says, "Shut up, Etler! They'll hear us!" She's laughing too, though, so I guess I'm all right. Damn, it feels good to have a best friend.

Next she takes me where the road curves a hard left because if it kept going straight, you'd drive right into the ocean. Joanna told me that a few years ago, some white boys from Westport forgot to turn their car when the road turned, so Bridgeport put three giant boulders there, to protect all the drug buyers from themselves. Now I guess these rocks are the Place, because as soon as we reach them, this young kid comes out of nowhere. He looks just like the kid in my favorite elementary book, *J.T.* The one about the bad little Harlem boy who makes friends with a one-eyed alley cat.

"Wanna cop?" he asks, his head level with Joanna's boobs.

"Yeah. Gimme a dime," Joanna says back to him, cool as fucking Fonzie.

Haloed by the streetlight, the kid slides a hand into his Adidas pants pocket. Then he palms out a bag the size of the lid on a fancy ring box. It's fat with shreddy dark stuff. Joanna licks her pointer finger to slide one five, then another, off her wad of bills. She's got all the time in the world.

The kid pinches the fives in their upper corners and snaps them so they're straight, holding them up in front of his eyes. Then he gives us a nod.

"Later," he says.

And he's gone. And we have a bag of pot. What the fuck? We have a bag of pot.

"Oh my God, Joanna! What do we do now?"

If I was Kim, I'd know what to do. She's just...*cool.* And that's why I steal her stuff. When I wear her clothes, it's a tiny bit like I'm Kim.

The best thing I stole from her is this pin I wear on my denim. It's got the Rolling Stones lips on it, and underneath, in blurry letters, it says "Stoned." Not Stone*s*, Stone*d*. What's cooler than that?

But with an actual bag of pot in front of me, I can't even try to be cool. It's useless. I'm totally that yippy cartoon dog at the chill bulldog's heels. Soon Jo'll reach a paw around and smack me.

But she doesn't.

"Let's go by the Zarzozas,'" she says, like I'm not a major embarrassment.

The Zarzozas are a bunch of brothers who make up half of "the guys." When you first hear their name, you think their story will be beautiful too. It's not. It's a flower gone rotten, all slimy and black. When Jo first told me about them, I stopped feeling so bad about my situation.

The oldest brother is thirty, but he never hangs out, so he doesn't count. The youngest brother is sixteen. His name is Tony, and he looks like Zorro. The middle brother is twenty-eight. He lives in the basement, and his name? It's fucked up. One day, after taking a wicked crap, Dad Zarzoza starts fighting with the middle brother. To win the fight, the dad grabs his son by the neck and pushes his head into the toilet—which the dad hadn't flushed. That brother's been called Shithead ever since.

There used to be a mother, but Jo doesn't know what happened to her. Oh, and Tony has the hots for Joanna. But she thinks he's gross. "I am not going out with a kid whose father doesn't flush it," is how she put it.

The D'agostinos are the other half of "the guys." They live down from the Zarzozas, on the ocean side of the street. Steve D'agostino, the guy Jo has a crush on, is fifteen. His brother Rich is twenty-five and too good for everyone, but he'll party with Steve and his friends when there's nothing else to do. Joanna points out their house as we walk by. It's tiny and gray, and I wonder how a father and two brothers can all fit inside it.

Jo says Mr. D'agostino owns a fishing company, which explains the lobster traps all over the lawn. "Their dad's out on the lobster boat most of the time," she says.

For some reason we both laugh at that. It becomes funnier and funnier until we're bent over, wheezing, and our sides hurt.

Up ahead, we hear different laughter, guy laughter. Four shapes loom out of the darkness like extras from the "Thriller" video. Their faces are in shadow, featureless as olives. All I can tell is they're white and male and wearing a lot of denim. "Woahhhh!" one of them says. Then there's more laughter.

Joanna has this crooked grin on, so the ghouls must be her friends. She slaps her hand on my back, and together we walk forward. Good, Cyndy. Good dog.

"Dudes," Jo says.

And suddenly we're surrounded by man-boys. I can tell which one is Tony Zarzoza. His hair is pitch black, and his lips and nose look royal. He'd be good to have as your boyfriend, if his dad wasn't a shit pervert.

"This is Cyndy," she says, tilting her chin at me.

None of them say hi. For two lifetimes, we just stand there—me with my eyes on the biggest guy's belly, them with their eyes wherever. I feel like I'm electrified, all crackly and glowing. This is *real* life, on a dark city street, surrounded by hoods. Fuckin' A.

Ever cool, Joanna breaks the silence.

"I copped," she says to the big guy. To Shithead.

"Good girl," he tells her. He reaches out and pinches her nipple through her shirt. And Joanna just jabs her shoulder at him, breaking off the pinch.

"Fucking *Shit*head!" she goes, but she's laughing. The nipple's standing out against her shirt, hard as a doorbell.

Then the dude with the *Miami Vice* hair and polo shirt is shoving his palm at Joanna. It's *gotta* be Rich D'agostino.

"Lemme have it," Rich says to Jo.

"Jesus. Chill, asshole," she says back, but she's sucking in her belly, squeezing her fingers into the pocket of her skin-tight Levi's. She pulls out the little baggie and hands it over.

Now watch: this'll be the moment they talk to me, wanting to know what kind of pot I like. Fuck! Why do I wear this Stoned button? All it does is make people ask questions I can't answer. When everyone starts moving, I run-skip ahead and fake deafness. Still, I catch slips of sentences.

"Who's got papers?"

"Anyone got a bowl?"

What do we need bowls for? I thought you *smoked* pot. Thank God I don't have to know, because I'm in my own bubble. I'm flying through Bridgeport air, through the fizziest night of my life.

"Where'd she get *those*?" I hear from behind me. They're talking about me. They're talking about...my *boobs*.

Joanna's words, "Shut *up,*" are drowned by more laughter. Like, sharp, razor laughter.

Five minutes later, we're at the Zarzozas'. Shithead goes first, leading us around the car on blocks, the upside-down armchair in the driveway. I'm at the back of the line, behind this chopstick of a kid. He must be Steve D'agostino. There's no streetlights or anything, so when he stops short, I bash right into his back.

"Hey, sorry," I tell him, and he actually turns and looks at me. And smiles.

"No prob."

His bangs are even longer than mine, all the way down

to his nose. When he tosses his head and his bangs swing sideways, you see long, long lashes and cow-brown eyes. Maybe he's cute. Maybe I get why Jo likes him.

When me and Steve get around back, the rest of the group is leaning on this huge dead tree that lies across the yard. I stand next to Steve in the perfect spot, where two limbs as thick as cans of soup form a V. I can't see anyone's face real good, only their outlines, so I don't know what's happening, exactly.

"Fucking *care*ful, man!" Jo says.

"Chill out and gimme yer lighter," a guy snaps back.

That's Rich. He's not the nicest guy. You can tell. But Joanna chills, or at least, she doesn't say anything back to him. I wonder what Mr. Azore's doing right now. I wonder what he'd think of how his twenty got spent.

Click-*shhhhhhh*. A face is lit with an orange glow. It's a big face, probably Shithead's. He's holding something up to his mouth, something shorter and wider than a cigarette. He's got the lighter sideways over it. I don't know what the fuck he's doing, 'cause he's holding the flame in just one spot. Shouldn't the thing be lit by now, for crap's sake? Finally the flame goes out. I can't see, but I can feel everyone's eyes fastened onto him.

"It's good shit," he croaks, in a voice that sounds like it hurts.

He hands the thing he's holding to Rich and then barks out a cough, which makes everyone but me crack up.

So this is getting stoned? And I'm supposed to know what I'm doing? Jesus. I better watch what the fuck Rich does.

When the mystery thing gets to me, I grab it from Tony's hand, like I've done this a zillion times. And I swear, it's like Satan's biting my fingertips.

"*Ooowww!* What the *fuck*?"

Those are the first words I say to these guys. Nice. Tony cough-laughs and pulls the thing—the boiling hot, little fucking metal pipe—away from me; I stick my burnt fingertips into my mouth. Was *Go Ask Alice* this stupid, before she turned cool? Couldn't she have given us directions?

"You gotta hold the bowl at the middle part, Cyndy. At the *glass* part. You ever smoked pot before?"

Tony's on to me. He knows what a loser I am. He totally smells my hot nervousness. But I cover it up with my Kim voice.

"Course I have."

"Sure you have."

Shithead peels off of the trunk and steps over to me, a greasy warmth coming off his body. Before I can tell how I feel about this, his hot dog fingers are clamped over my mouth and a metal circle's pushed between my lips. It clacks against my teeth.

"Okay, lock your lips around it. When I light the bowl, inhale. But *don't open your mouth.*"

My heart is pumping blood so fast, I can hear it skidding through my veins. This moment is vital. If these guys don't like me, I'll never get to come back. I'll be stuck in Monroe forever, in that devil house with Jacque. I have to get this right. I *will* get this right.

I tighten my lips and lift my eyes. Shithead's face is so close he could take a bite outta me. With a click of the lighter, he's all lit up. He's got shark-teeth.

After my father died, but before my mother met Jacque, Kim and I would play this game called Damsel in Distress. A villain would capture a damsel and tie her to the railroad tracks. She would scream, "Help! Help!" and then, right before the train hit, a hero would show up to save her. Kim always got to be the damsel, of course. And I always had to be the villain. And the hero. When I pictured what the villain would look like, Shithead's face was pretty much what I saw.

He brings the flame to the end of the pipe and I inhale thorny smoke.

"Hold it in! Hold it *in*!" he's saying, his face even closer than before.

From behind him I hear cheering and a "Yeeaaaah!"

There's a lumberjack in my throat trying to ax his way out, but I hold it in. I hold it 'til an invisible kick in my back knocks me forward, slamming the smoke out of my lungs. My hands catch my knees, and I crouch there and hack. I hack out flames and axed-up throat chunks.

But after that there's this feeling of...well...*winning*. I smoked pot, and the man-boys cheered. I'm here in

Bridgeport, in this blue ink night, so crisp you could snap it in half. I'm surrounded by tough guys, cool guys, where Jacque could never find me.

So this is what it's like, getting high. Getting high equals getting safe. Yeah. Now I see why everybody wants it.

2

GUYS MUST WEAR SHIRTS—GIRLS MUST WEAR BRAS

When I'm done hacking up a lung, I stand and lean back against the tree. Its bark is slick as I rub my hands over the trunk. Everyone's silent, but I know they're all watching me. They're seeing how I'm the same as them, tight jeans and dirty shoes, and how I got stoned. They're wishing I'd stay here. I turn around to tell them yes—*I'll stay here with you! I will!*—but they're not looking at me. They're not looking at anything. Joanna's lighting the bowl and sucking on it, and Tony's facing Joanna. The rest of the circle has their heads down, like heavy flowers on weak stems.

I don't know what to do, so I look at the ground and study our shoes. There are four pairs of scuffed-up work boots. One of the pairs is small, for a girl. There's one pair of Topsiders, and a pair of wet gray Keds. My Keds look like baby shoes next to the work boots.

When the pipe comes around the circle again, Steve fits it into my hand and lights it for me. This time, when I bend over to choke afterward, I'm not so surprised. This time, nobody cheers. The stars shine; the moon grins. Eventually everyone creaks themselves up and lumbers like dinosaurs toward the Zarzoza house.

Down in the basement, behind a dungeon door, is Shithead's room. A curtain cuts the room in half, hiding whatever's behind it. There's a cot against one wall, the creaky, uncomfortable kind. That's where I sit, between Steve and Shithead. Our butts press into the scratchy army blanket.

Voices start and stop; laughter jumps and falls. But none of it is mine. What can I say to make them laugh? "Hey guys! Did you get a load of my shoes?" I need to do or say something. I need to earn my place. But since I have zero ideas, I'm fucked. As soon as they talk to me, they'll learn: there's no reason to want me here.

I've gotta avoid my trial.

"I don't feel very good," I garble out.

I push up from the cot and go to the curtain, sliding through the opening. On the other side, I'm better. Out of the spotlight. Alone.

Through the glow from the curtain slit, I see Shithead's stuff: a jumbo-size water bed, a side table, and a small rectangular window with the glass painted black. On the nightstand there's a magazine with the pages folded back; the page facing up shows a naked lady. So, of course, I tiptoe over to it. The lady's sucking her own nipple! Is that what boys want girls to do? I flip the magazine over all quiet, so they won't think I was looking. Then I just stand there, frozen, as the voices keep rumbling from the other side of the curtain.

Okay. They're not listening to me. I kneel on the edge of the water bed, where the hard wooden box meets the rolling rubber mattress. Then I lie down, and it's like a whole body sigh. The waves shift underneath me. Safe. I'm safe.

There's a stretch of quiet that's broken by gunshot laughter. And then the curtain parts, shooting an arrow of light across the room. I freeze and hold my breath. God, let me seem asleep. Don't make me talk to anyone. As soon as I open my mouth, they're gonna say, "Jo, get that girl outta here. Come back when she's gone."

Through my lashes, I see the thin arrow of light. Then it's gone. It's dark, and someone's in here with me. I sense it: a presence, thick and silent.

The someone moves toward me while the voices keep going. My heart is pounding out Morse code as the someone lies down next to me, kicking up rubber-mattress waves. My eyes are closed, my breathing's quiet. *My Bonnie lies over the ocean.* I never liked that song when we had to sing it in music class—because how could she be lying *over* an ocean? Now, I think I get it.

The someone's hand is on my stomach. The hand starts moving up.

They have to like me.

I have to seem asleep.

My Bonnie lies over the sea. It's not a bad song, really. The hand is up to my bra, heavy-thumbing me through the thin, fake silk. The thumb is rough, and my belly tumbles backward. I'm breathing quiet. I'm not *letting* this happen, because I'm asleep. I'm dreaming about elementary music class.

My Bonnie lies over the ocean, now bring back my Bonnie to me.

Now two hands are on me. They're pulling my shirt up, scrunching it under my chin. Thick fingers are burrowing beneath the underwire of my bra. They're pushing the underwire up and over my boobs. The hands spread over them like spiders.

Bring back, bring back, bring back my Bonnie to me, to me. The hands belong to Shithead. I know it because when the head moves down and the mouth latches onto me, I flick my eyes open. The hair is dark; the body is big. Too big for a teenager.

My body's a blender on high. Sparks and tingles are zinging all over me, from my z-z to my boobs, like Pop Rocks. I can't believe this is happening to me. I don't know if I want this happening to me. No, I don't *know* that this is happening to me. Because I'm asleep. I am stoned and asleep with my Bonnie.

A door slams upstairs somewhere, and the mouth unlatches with a pop. Shithead sits up, hard and fast, which turns the water bed into a tidal wave. I'm choking on the roll of cloth and underwire as my uncovered boobies turn cold, as the gummy stamp of spit burns into me. I need to pull my shirt down. I need to rub the slime off my boob, maybe 'til it bleeds. But since I'm asleep, I can't move.

Shithead's palm lands flat on my stomach with a slap. He leans into my face and says one word.

"Hosebag."

His footsteps cross the room, back through the curtain, as I curl up like a shrimp. From the other side of the curtain I hear a question, clear as water.

"What's she doing?"

And an answer.

"Lying there."

Not sleeping. *Lying* there. I squeeze my eyes tighter, squinching out thoughts of my plain white boobs. If I'm not asleep, then that was my choice. Like, I *let* Shithead do that. God, no. I'm just a deadish body. I lie on the water bed, my boobies unguarded. Minutes tick past.

I guess I'm safe. Nobody's thinking about me. My hands are itching to cover up my top. I'm just gonna—

The curtain jerks open, cutting off my thought. There's a laugh. In the light, I see Rich D'agostino. Then the curtains fall back together and it's dark again. I lie as still as a sleeping girl can.

He talks to me normal, as if I was awake.

"Hi, Cyndy. Whatchya doin' back here?"

Rich sits on the edge of the bed, then wraps his fingers around my boobies like he owns them. Which makes my nips tug tight. Which makes Rich laugh, like I finally thought of something funny to say. Then he moves his palms on me, which makes me feel soft and clean and empty. They make it hard to breathe slow, like a sleeping girl would. Like a girl who wouldn't let this—like a girl who wouldn't *like* this.

Rich lies his body down along mine. It feels so different from when Jacque does. It still feels scary, but Rich at least is cute, and he has magician hands. When he pushes my shirt higher, my bra flips over and the underwire lands on my chin. It's embarrassing, but I can't fix it, since I'm asleep.

Rich's hand moves lower. His thumb is under my jeans, and his fingers start pulling at the top button. It doesn't pop open so he gets mad at it. He jams both hands down my waistband and starts ripping. The first button pops. And then the whole row.

Rich's breath is going faster. His hands are on my sides, trying to pull my Levi's down, but my hips won't let go of my jeans. My boobs are bouncing around, helpless, but I've gotta seem asleep. If I'm letting this happen, Jo will *never* bring me back here. I do a little "Uh?" to sound realistic.

My jeans are totally stuck. So is my breath; so is my brain. Even my *jeans* don't know if they want what's happening. But Rich—Rich knows what he wants. Still, even with two hands, he can't peel off my Levi's. Panting like a dog, he pushes my feet to my butt, making my knees bend up, and he scratch-curls his fingers into the sides of my Levi's. Then, with one sharp yank, my pants are halfway down my thighs.

With Rich's knees on my feet, I'm a prisoner. I can't straighten my legs, or push myself away. But Rich stops moving. All the motion dies. I'm cricket-kneed on a water bed, a six-foot man on my toes; from thigh to shoulder, I'm naked. Except for Kim's fancy underwear.

Rich is totally still. He must be staring at me. I can picture what he'd see: a blur of hair over a closed-eye face. A scrunched shirt and bra dividing head from boobies. A belly and ribbon-tie underwear. The underwear suddenly feels about the size of a safety pin. Maybe that's what he's staring at. He can't believe how cute they are.

He must be done thinking now because he presses his hand—which is big as a stop sign—over my hip. It feels like an electric shock, like something very good and bad is about to happen.

But Rich moves his hand away, and the electricity shorts out. Then there's a tickle on my hip, and a wave of cool skims my z-z. He—he untied my underwear. He leans over me and undoes the other side, too. Am I about to have sex? Do I *want* to have sex? Is this how Jo passed the test and got in?

Like he can read my mind, Rich starts his laugh again, then cups his massive hand over my z-z. *Oh God, oh God.* It's the opposite of when Jacque—of when I lock up, of when Jacque gets in my room. That's when I make myself hard, a stainless steel padlock. Then nothing can actually happen to me. I just lock up and go to God. But if I *wasn't* made of metal, if I *could* scream, my mother would burst in and save me. I know she would. If she saw what he does, she wouldn't say that I'm trying to get attention or that I'll make a great actress someday. She'd save me. But when Jacque—when I'm locked up—I can't scream. Padlocks don't make noise once they get snapped shut.

But none of that matters right now. Right now, with Rich's hand, I feel swirly and alive.

Because Rich is moving his fingers, and it feels *good*.

I'm naked on this dirty bed.

But Rich is gorgeous. And so is his hand.

There's a bunch of strangers a cloth curtain away.

But his hand isn't Jacque's as it windshield-wipers me.

I feel melty, like caramel, like I'm floating away from—

"Hey, Dick. How's it going back there?" a guy calls.

The voice is a bolt of lightning. It cuts the dark and shows me what's really going on. My body's not caramel, it's plastic. My butt fat is flattened on my panties, and my legs are spread ugly, held open like a car door by Rich's arm. My boobs should be called something gross now, like "titties."

Rich doesn't answer the question. Instead, he pushes a raw finger up my z-z, and all of a sudden, he *is* Jacque.

"You like that, Cyndy?" he asks, his lips right next to my ear.

I forgot how to sleep-breathe. Now I'm just lying here. Letting him.

"You like that, you little hosebag? Hosemonkey."

He pushes his finger around, breathing heavy. Heavy

enough for both of us. And then he's sitting up. The water bed shoves me back and forth as he wipes his finger on my belly, and then he's gone. I'm alone behind the curtain again, just me and the magazine lady, sucking her own tittie.

"Anyone wants her, she's ready," Rich says like a carnival barker.

"How old is she?" asks another guy.

"Thirteen," Joanna says.

Someone hocks and spits.

"Jailbait."

So I'm "jailbait." Which I guess means nobody wants me. I thought 501s were the right pants to get me in, but maybe not. I must need some zip-flys.

3

KNOCK ON ALL DOORS BEFORE ENTERING

It's hard going back to prison after you've been free. After you've been to Bridgeport. Being trapped in my house sucks even more now that I know what I'm missing. So I'm ready to fight, which is what I'm doing right now. Fighting. And it's about time.

My mother puts her fingers in her ears when Jacque decides to hunt me. Kim does too, when she's here. They're all, *la-la-la-I-can't-HEAR-you!* But they'd have to be fucking deaf to miss the show tonight. And the show is me saying, FUCK YOU. Because I've got Bridgeport out there waiting for me. I've got an escape hatch, where people who *get* me are waiting. So finally, fuck you.

I beat Jacque to my room and jerk the thumb latch out of my colonial-days door handle. Then I slam the door in his face. He's right there on the other side of it, but he can't get to me without the thumb latch. He's a wasp, clacking on a window. *Ha!* I win.

But he'll get in here, watch. He'll get a knife to lever the handle open, or else he'll bust the door down. So I'm getting out the other way. I throw open my window, rip the screen off, and slip through like I'm greased. My feet slide a little on the ledge, and I look down to see what I would've landed on, if I'd kept sliding: a slab of concrete. It's the septic tank lid, pressed tight into the ground. It looks like my father's grave.

In case you haven't guessed, we *really* don't talk about stuff in my house. But if you knew who my father was, you wouldn't *believe* I have to live with scuzzballs like Jacque and his kids. I don't know what kind of crazy my mother was to marry Jacque. Or maybe crazy's not the word. Maybe desperate is.

My mother met Jacque at Parents Without Partners, after my father died. You'd think she would have been grossed out by his doody breath and French accent, but no. My mother goes for weird shit, I guess. Plus we were about to get kicked out of our apartment for not paying rent. Plus Jacque had a house we could live in. So now we live with him.

But I still say she's crazy. Because she was crazy when she married my father too. Would you marry your college professor? Okay, maybe you would. But what if he was like thirty years older than you? Seriously, my father was married *three times* before he met my mother. He had a whole other family before us—and his kids from that first family? They're older than my mother! See? *Crazy*.

But my father's fame canceled out his age, I guess. He was this big-time classical music composer, Alvin Derald Etler. Seriously, look him up. He was a mega big deal, which made my mother mega too, I guess. But when Kim was five and I was one, my dad got really sick and dropped dead. And then everything *sucked* for my mega-mother, the twenty-seven-year-old widow. That brand of suck lasted a few years, until Jacque came along. With Jacque, at least she had a roof over her head. But if my mother snagged a bigwig her first time around, why'd she take a loser the second time?

You know, falling on this septic tank slab under my window isn't a bad idea. If I landed the right way, it could solve all my problems. I'd be gone from this house, and maybe my mother and sister would finally believe what I keep telling them. Only then, it'd be too late for them to do anything about it.

I can totally picture them kneeling at my grave, right next to my father's, and banging their foreheads on my tombstone.

CYNDY DREW ETLER
WE DIDN'T KNOW WE LOVED HER
'TIL SHE WAS GONE

Kim would cry and cry, but my mother would wheel around and tear into Jacque, who, for some reason, would be standing right behind them. Then she'd beat the living crap out of him.

I'm picturing my mom and Kim sobbing when a **BAM!** snaps me back from grave-side no-life to window-ledge real life. And what the *fuck*? My bedroom door punches open, and my doorway's full of Jacque and his vein-bursting face. There's a blast of voices, then Jacque's hand rockets through the open window and clamps the fat of my arm. He's dragging me back through the window, into my room. My arms and head are inside now, facing that dirty pink carpet I loved so much when I first moved here. But my legs are still outside, and my middle's getting crushed by the windowsill. Jacque keeps pulling and voices keep screaming as my legs thump through the window and my head slams into the floor.

I go blank for a second, then rip out a howl like you've never fucking heard. You know that sound Dr. David Banner makes when he turns into the Hulk? Mine is *so* much worse than that. It almost blocks out my mother's screams—"Stop this! Stop trying to get attention!" And Kim's—"I saw her out there! She was gonna jump!" My howl from hell scares them away from me. All of them, even Jacque. They clear the fuck out and I'm alone again, hate skidding through my veins. And it feels *good*. Today, I stopped him.

I feel so fucking good, I decide I can just leave this house. I know where Bridgeport is, ten exits up the highway. I'll get there somehow. I'll work it out. I mean, the hate makes me *that* stupid.

The hellfire in my brain gives me orders: "Cigarettes. Tiptoe. Front door." I get there quick and quiet, 'cause they're all still hiding from me. The soft click of the door behind me, the cold smash of October on my skin—they're gas on the fire. I'm blind with hate as I run, stumbling down that gutted driveway, racing toward the plan that I don't have yet. Ten exits. Twenty miles.

It's cold, and the stars look like they're in 3-D. The death-smell of rotting leaves makes a thumbprint in my memory. I'm not crying anymore, and finally I'm not screaming. I can hear the **clack-clack** of stones beneath my feet in this dried riverbed of a road.

Usually when I run from that house I bring my Walkman, because Zeppelin is a drug and Floyd is a magic carpet. But the fury tonight didn't leave me time to grab headphones. So I'm alone out here. There are no lights on in my grown-up-friend Dawn's house, no lights in the hermit guy's house. Just the blue-death glow of TV in the old couple's front window. It's dark, and there are no other houses for half a mile. The cold takes a bite from my skin.

Once I'm past the mailboxes, past the boulder at Shady Lane, I slow down a little. I crunch past the house where I used to hate babysitting—the Earwigs, with their red-headed kids and their science-experiment butterflies in the freezer. If Pat Earwig sees me, she'll call the cops.

Just past the Earwigs' is this crumble-down shack. I'm telling you, there's something in the woods there. I don't know what, but I can feel it. Head down, hurry up, get through to the white house with the white fence. It's all lit up like a party or something—who lives that way?—and **boom**, I'm at the end of Shady Lane.

You couldn't pay me enough to take the long, dark driveway up to Chalk Hill Middle School right now. It would make better hiding, but God only knows what's up there at night. Fawn Hollow Elementary is low and wide open, but it will have to do. There's nowhere to hide in this stupid playground, but who else is out here? Nobody. Just me.

Pressed against the side of Fawn Hollow, I stop. The burn of the lighter on my thumb feels almost good; so does the punch of a Marlboro. I feel the cold grate of brick against my back; I see the white-blue glow of the stars. I hear silence; I taste Marlboro. It's midnight in Monroe, Connecticut. No one's around. No one's awake. And no one has come after me. I'm alone, just me and my galloping heart.

When my heart slows down, my thoughts come back. They remind me that Bridgeport is ten exits, twenty miles away. That Joanna is five miles, two parents, and a doorbell-at-midnight away.

So. I'll sit out there 'til I feel the dew, then I'll walk back home.

I have nowhere else to go.

4

NO TALKING IN THE BATHROOMS

The little shack house burned down. You know, the one on Shady Lane? By the creepy stretch of woods? No one knows how it caught on fire. I'm telling you, that street *is* shady.

I'd escaped to my neighbor Dawn's for the day when we smelled something weird. We went out in her backyard to see what was up, and this gray smoke was pouring into the sky from somewhere close. We put her kids in the stroller and followed the smoke past the boulder, past the Earwigs', and right to the front of the shack, which was a box of flames. We stood there and stared as it popped and spit.

After a while, old Pat Earwig crunched over the hill in her station wagon. You could see her eyeballs, bugged out and big as goose eggs, through the windshield. That woman hauled ass into her driveway, and five minutes later the fire truck showed up. Well, watching the shack fire was fun while it lasted. And now Pat Earwig has to live next to a giant charcoal briquette.

What wasn't fun was going back to my mother's house. I've been spending a lot of time at Dawn's, for obvious reasons. But when Dawn and them go out as a family, I'm not invited. I mean, who's gonna pay my way? And I can't stay with them full-time, because it would be kidnapping or something. Dawn could get in trouble with my mother.

But I don't know. That seems bogus to me, 'cause my half-sister, Shirley? She's one of my father's first kids, who lives in Virginia. She has a daughter in high school named Julie. And Julie has this friend who moved in with them, because her father was so mean or her family moved away and she wanted to stay in the same high school or something. How come that's not kidnapping? People let other teenagers stay with them all the time, just not *me*. I must be so annoying that Dawn only wants me around part-time.

At least this weekend I get to go with Jo to Bridgeport and see Steve. Steve D'agostino—did I tell you? We're going out now! I can't even believe it. I have an actual boyfriend, and he lives in Bridgeport! He's so skinny that when we walk down the street, we must look like Kermit and Miss Piggy, but other than that, he's totally perfect. When we're together, he holds my hand and gives me cigarettes. And he loves making out. I just wish he wasn't so drooly.

What sucks is I can only see him when I go to Bridgeport

with Jo. He can't come to Monroe 'cause he has no way to get here. But we talk on the phone all the time, and he totally cares how fucked my life is.

Dawn lets me hang out in her room by myself to call him, and it's heaven, lying on her clean-smelling bed and looking at all her porcelain dolls with their hopeful faces and frilly dresses. Every doll has a different hairstyle, like a thousand blond ringlets or dark hair coiled into cinnamon buns. Lying there looking at those dolls and waiting for Steve to pick up, I almost feel like I can dive into a doll and *become* her, clean and pretty, living on a shelf in Dawn's house.

Then Steve picks up the phone, and his voice makes me forget about being porcelain. He does this thing I'll never forget. He says to me, "Hold on." Next thing I know, the opening bar of "Wish You Were Here" is playing through the phone. The banjo twang makes my stomach drop. There's no sound more lonely than a banjo, but Steve playing that song into the phone is the anti-lonely. There's that rumbly cough in the background, and as the song rolls on I'm frozen, trying to make time stop. Steve starts singing the chorus part, like he wishes *I* was *there*. For the rest of the song, we just listen together and breathe. I never had a moment so perfect.

In exchange for my having Steve as a boyfriend, Joanna's acting weird. She had a crush on Steve before, okay. But I asked her! I asked if she minded that we liked each other, and she said don't worry about it. But still. She's acting a little...I don't know. Quiet, or something. Which makes me feel...I don't know. Scared, or something.

It's Thursday night, late, and I've got to get my stuff together for Bridgeport this weekend. My good clothes are in the dryer, which means whoever is in the TV room is gonna hear me get them out. When I snuck in from Dawn's earlier this evening, I could hear the TV on, but now it's past my stepbrother's bedtime and there's light under my stepsister's door, which means my mother and Jacque are watching TV together. Gross.

I've been waiting for them to go to bed so I could get my clothes, but it's almost midnight and I've got to get up for school. So I creep down the stairs and whisper the laundry door open.

No dice. Jacque's French accent punctures my hope.

"Vhat're you doeenk, Cinny?"

I bet he saw my clothes in the dryer and has been waiting for me to come get them. Vulture.

"Nothing," I mumble.

"Cyndy, answer his question."

Ever-helpful, that's my mother.

"Leave me alone, Ma."

"Vhat are you *doeenk,* Cinny?"

The plastic sofa creaks as he pushes himself up, all amped for a fight.

"I'm *doing nothing*!"

BAM! And it's on. The door to the laundry room is ripped open, and he's huffing booze fumes right at me.

"You don talk do me that way!"

Like a hunted animal, I go on instinct, not thought. I lunge into the tiny downstairs bathroom. There's only one exit, and it's now full of Jacque.

"I was *talk*ing to my *mother*!"

My voice, to him, is a shove. And he's on me. He wraps a hand around my arm, and his beef-palm connects with my face. Once, twice, again and again. Through the tornado, I see his smile.

I try to twist away, so he squeezes harder. Pulling my head down to dodge another blow, I spot my mother in the doorway. Salvation.

"Help me, Ma," I bleat. "Ma!"

My mother stands still. Her eyes are quiet, her mouth is soft. She doesn't say a word. She just watches.

I'm so gone.

The Shady Lane shack is where I end up, 'cause where else am I gonna go? I'm trying to avoid the charred spots, to stay clean. The firemen got the flames out before the whole ground floor went up, and I'm hoping they saved a circle big enough to lie down on.

I feel weird, hyper and exhausted all at once. My backpack is gonna be my pillow. It's not the most comfortable, but it's something. Lying back on it, I've got everything I need: my music, my cigarettes, and a place to hide. As long as the roof doesn't fall in on me, I'm okay for tonight.

It's gotta be, what, two in the morning? Perfect time to lie back and sleep. But tomorrow night and the next, where am I gonna stay? Well, shit. I may not know where I'll be for my fourteenth birthday in two weeks, but I know where I *won't* be. I won't be in that house.

Maybe I can stay with Steve. I could work for Mr. D'agostino on his lobster boat, keep Steve and me in cigarettes. Maybe even eventually Mr. D'agostino would adopt me. Yeahhh.

I can feel the back and forth of the waves rocking Mr. D'agostino's boat. I hear the **TIP**-*slap* of the water against the sides, and the **grrrrr** of other boats' motors as they pass. They're rushing past fast. Their tires grind through the gravel, flinging it sideways, and—wait, what? That wasn't a boat whizzing past, that was a dream. No, that was a car! A real car, racing up Shady Lane in the middle of the night!

Who the fuck could that be? None of these old people would have a visitor at 2:00 a.m. That car has to be after me. But who'd be *driving* here? I'm okay, though. No one knows where I am. So I'm just gonna lie here 'til the sun comes up, take the bus to school, find a dime and call Steve. He'll get me to Bridgeport, and I'll be rescued. Everything's fine.

Everything's—oh my God, *footsteps*? Fucking, heavy *breathing*?! My heart's a guitar string pulled too tight; my chest twangs ugly. He found me.

"*Cyn*dy!"

The footsteps have stopped. The air is silent. I smell burnt house. Gravel crunches twice, and a jellybean of light pops up on a blackened window square.

"Cyndy, it's Dawn! Are you in there?"

"Dawn!" If she hadn't heard my voice, she'd have heard my twanging heart.

"Come on, Cyndy! Rudy's at your mom's house!"

Rudy? Who the fuck is Rudy? "I'm not going back there, Dawn."

The silence gives us both time to think. A wind kicks up; it rustles the dry leaves overhead. They sound like shaking dice, like gambling dice. Dawn crunches closer.

"C'mon, Cyndy," she says. "I'm not going to make you go back."

I got found, the story of my life. So really, I have no say. I push myself off the charcoal floor, grab my backpack, and step outside.

"Who's Rudy?" I ask.

"The Monroe police youth officer. Your mom called the cops on you."

"The *cops*? Are at my *house*? Looking for *me*?"

"Come on. You're staying at our house tonight."

Like a fish on a hook, I'm yanked back up the hill toward

Jacque and that house. Dawn slings her arm around my shoulder and goes, "I'll make you some Swiss Miss." Which would feel great, if it was a long-term commitment.

5

NO OVERALLS OR WHITE T-SHIRTS IN GROUP

On the morning after my big, tough runaway, when I get off the bus at school, there's no Jo. She's not in her usual spot, sitting on the dumpster lid, waiting for me. I find her in the smoking pit with the renegade kids from Beacon Falls, the ones who get bussed up to Masuk 'cause their town's too small for a high school.

She's leaning, super-chill, on the slanted wall behind her. Me, I can't be un-chill enough.

"We still going tonight?" I jackhammer out.

"Yeah," she says back.

She scans the pit with her eyes, then points a finger at her denim's front pocket. I can't think of *any*thing other than getting to Bridgeport, but still, I raise my brows. She spreads open the pocket so I can see what's in there: a brass tube, thick as a thumb, with a green metal cup at the end. A little pipe. So we're gonna get high *before* Bridgeport tonight? Fuckin' A.

I can feel her eyes on my face. But Joanna's so cool, she doesn't ask me any questions. I mean, I know I don't look right. My eyes are blue-circled like lunar eclipses, from being up all night and from Jacque. But Jo leaves it alone.

After school, on the bus to her house, I go, "I can't go back to my house, man," and she just says, "All right."

Soon as we walk through her front door, she's yelling. "Dad! Can we stay Sunday night too? You can drive us to school Monday? It's okay with Cyndy's parents."

Mr. Azore's voice comes back, "Okay."

Done. Just like that. We're staying in Bridgeport Friday, Saturday, *and* Sunday night, like we actually live there. And my mother will have no idea how to get me. As if she'd even try, now that last night's drama—*My daughter ran away! Help me, Mr. Policeman!*—is over.

Besides. When Dawn went and told Youth Officer Rudy I was staying at her house last night, he told my mother to let me "cool off" there until Monday. And if a man in uniform says it's a good idea, that settles it. I'm safe, at least for the weekend. I have to call Dawn and tell her I'm staying at my best friend's place, instead. But I don't have to tell her *which* place…

See? My life is all working out, like God snapped his wrist and flung open a photo-accordion of possibilities. I just had to—no fucking around—leave that house. I had to prove I *meant* it. Now that I have, He's totally gonna save me. I don't know yet if it'll be Dawn's or Jo's or Steve's or what, but he'll put me in somebody's house, where I'll be safe and people will *like* me. For sure.

It's like, as soon as we cross into Bridgeport, every pore on my body opens and all this air rushes in. Even though you could get shot on any street corner, I feel safe. I wish I knew how to tell Jo's parents how thankful I am that they brought me here. I'm gonna ask God to do something nice for them too.

Jo snagged one of her dad's T-shirts for me to wear, because mine was pretty skanky. It's a big white V-neck with nubbles in the armpits, the kind of shirt dads wear on weekends for doing plumbing and stuff. It's big enough to knot at my middle, but I like wearing it long, like a dress. With my denim jacket over it and my Levi's underneath, I look like one of the Outsiders.

When Joanna and me are heading for the Zarzozas', it hits me: I'm not the scrappy sidekick anymore, all nervous and stupid. I'm as fuck-it as Jo is. We're parallel, like Ponyboy and Johnny. Not good enough for—but way better than—the pretty, happy people.

So when we're walking now, we don't need to talk. We're cool to just listen to our footsteps. We're in Bridgeport, we're out in the night, we're together. The moon's a purple scoop in a Cinderella sky.

We always sit in the same arrangement at the Zarzozas', like those hollow stacking dolls that only fit together in one order. I sit on the cot with Steve on my left and Shithead on my right. Jo and Tony sit across from us on the chairs that leak gray stuffing. The only missing doll is Rich.

We're smoking a joint tonight. To me it seems like just a hot little sliver of paper. It's so thin, I can't even feel it touching my mouth. And I still don't know how to suck it right. But I hear the pot popping, and the paper sizzles against my lips, so I guess I got a hit…?

God, just please let some smoke come out when I *exhaaaaale*…thank you. Thank you for making them not watch me. For making Steve scoot closer to me. For making me feel like I maybe sort of belong.

Tony brings the joint to his lips and inhales with tiny sucks. He closes his eyes and mouth for a second, and then huffs out. When he leans his head against the wall, Joanna and Shithead do too. They look blissed out, like the wall behind them is a feather pillow. They must be super baked, 'cause nobody's talking about smoking anymore. I guess we're supposed to listen to the death metal thumping out of the boom box.

I pull down the hem of Mr. Azore's shirt, making it a perfect line across my thighs. When I pull it extra hard, the V of the neck stretches so low you can see the top of my boobs. I want to know if Steve's noticing, but I can't turn and check. He has to think I'm just, you know, fiddling. Man, this big white T-shirt is awesome. Jo needs to get me a stash of these.

"Hey, wanna get outta here?"

At least, that's what I think I hear, but the music's pretty loud. I turn my head and there's Steve, a half-inch away from my nose. He *is* noticing. He says it again.

"Wanna go?"

He's looking at me. Right in my eyes. A lead brick drops in my belly. Go where? And...get out of here *how*? I mean, Bridgeport is big and dangerous. Shouldn't we have to ask somebody first?

Steve's still looking at me, still smiling. God, he actually *likes* me. Like, I could actually be *wanted* here.

"Um, 'kay." It's the best I can do.

Steve creaks up from the cot, then puts a hand out for me. It takes me about five minutes to stand, since I can only push up from the cot with my left hand. Because my right hand is being held by a boy. A cute boy, who *belongs*. Who could make me belong too, if he tells everybody I'm his. Me and this boy, we walk up the stairs, out of the Zarzoza house, and into the night.

Steve's house is all brown inside. The walls are made of fake wood. Mr. D'agostino must get so much blue out on the ocean, he doesn't want color when he's home.

He's out catching lobsters, I bet. Even though it's late-*late* night. Because he's definitely not here. You'd know if anyone else was home, because Steve's house is teeny. I wonder if, when one of them has to poop, the other two D'agostinos leave. Otherwise, in a house this small, they'd basically be all in the same room for it.

Steve has no mom. She died when he was little, so it's always been just Steve and Rich and their dad. Doesn't that seem weird? Like aren't only dads supposed to die, and moms get to live? But Steve's dad may as well have died, because he's totally not around. Ever since Steve was a little kid, he says, his dad's been out on the boat all the time. And when he's home all he does is drink and think about his dead wife. So frigging sad. Sometimes I wonder what God's thinking.

It's easy to tell what Steve's thinking, though, bringing me to his empty house. He's thinking about…you know. And I kinda wish he wasn't. He opens the back door and we're in the kitchen, which is jam-packed with a table, four chairs, and a dark brown fridge. I'm across the kitchen in two steps, pulling out a grandma-looking chair, all metal legs and brown and orange vinyl cushion. But I don't get to sit because Steve says something scary.

"Come see my room."

When I look at Steve, it's like he's a different kid. His hair is *mega*-greasy, and when did he get this skinny? He's looking back at me, like, super serious, and I have this realization: this is the first time I've seen Steve with a light on. This is how he's always looked. I just didn't know it.

Good thing I've got that chair to hold me up. I'm death-gripping it, both hands, as I turn away from Steve and study how truly mini his house is. You could fit this whole house into my bedroom in Monroe, almost. Where the fuck will they put me, when Steve's dad adopts me?

Steve's still looking at me.

"Yeah, so what's your room like?" I say, 'cause I have to say something.

I follow him through a fake-wood door, and we're in a living room. No windows, a big TV, and a cable box. MTV! But no MTV for me, because Steve's at another door. He pushes it in six inches before **clunk**, it stops. It must be blocked by his bed. But Steve doesn't even need to turn sideways to get through. He's a living toothpick. I try to sideways myself in, and the doorknob jams in my flab. Like I said, Kermit the Frog and Miss Piggy.

Steve's kicking some clothes into a corner, so I have a minute to scope the place out. Instead of brown, Steve's room is black. Mostly. It's black and DayGlo orange and yellow, with a purple lightbulb in the ceiling. You know what? I can get past skinniness to hang out in a room this cool. Glow-in-the-dark paint and a dad who's never home? I'll sleep standing in the closet if I have to. Just let me stay.

There's a Metallica tapestry hung on a slant over the

bed. I'm staring at it so I don't have to look at Steve, whose bed creaks as he lies down.

I'm like, scared. I left all my toughness on Joanna's street. It's back there leaning on a stop sign, smoking a cigarette. Here, in this empty house, I've got no tough at all.

After the bed creaks, the silence is long. Steve is the one to break it, by pressing the play button on his stereo. Wind comes rushing out of his speakers. I know this sound like a baby knows a heartbeat. It's Floyd, "Shine On You Crazy Diamond." It's our album.

I sit on the edge of his bed as a guitar moves in with the wind. Steve pushes himself next to me. There's a pinkie finger of space between us.

I need a pep talk. Like, *What the fuck is wrong with you? You've made out with Steve a ton. Like, three times. Quit being such a loser.*

Weird notes from a piccolo, maybe, swerve out of the speakers, and my head talks back to me.

We're alone in this house. Anything could happen. Any*thing.*

My stomach feels funny again. Steve's moving his face, putting it in front of mine. I mean, *right* in front. I can smell the moon and the Marlboro on his skin. I close my eyes and he presses his lips onto mine.

If Steve says you're his, you're in.

The guitar roils as Steve pushes his fighting slug of a tongue into my mouth. The piccolo's gone, but Steve's hands aren't. And I'm not nervous anymore. We're frantic as his hands move over my cotton-covered boobs and hips. His body feels boney on top of me, but his hands feel good. They're stronger than they look as they unpop the buttons on my 501s. Just like his brother did in the Zarzozas' basement the night we met.

Everything's moving quickly, and the guitar starts screaming, like I do, when I'm trapped by Jacque. My head is all splintered as Steve's hand slides down. It's too much. I'm seeing Jacque. I'm hearing music. I'm feeling Steve, whose fingers are at my triangle, which feels really scary and good. The guitar plucks out each note from "Shine On You Crazy Diamond."

The music is safe. If I concentrate on the music, maybe I can switch to just hearing and feeling, not thinking. The guitar and the piccolo and some kind of harp, they're criss-crossing each other like DNA. Like the beginning of everything. It's phenomenal and impossible, like Steve's fingers in my jeans.

"Wanna do it?"

The music turns to buzzing, as if Floyd is waiting for my answer, too. Steve's fingers are still in the pudding under my jeans, but everything feels cold now. My fingers unlatch from his shoulders, and my arms thud back to the mattress.

"I just..." I finally get out.

The music spirals off with downward notes.

"I don't think I'm ready," I say, as the final note dies.

The tape ends. The play button pops up on the stereo, and **SNAP**. It's over.

6

NO BORROWING MONEY, CANDY, OR CIGARETTES

After everything turned weird with Steve last night, I was psyched to get back to Jo's. We have twenty whole hours to just eat, sleep, and watch TV. We don't even have to hide in a locked bedroom. We can hang out right in the living room.

It's just me and Jo until way later, 'cause the guys are vampires. It's like they don't exist until after 9:00 p.m. We're not even supposed to talk about them if the sun's out. But I can't help it. I have to tell her about last night.

"Yeah, so Steve brought me to his house."

Joanna picks up her mom's cigarettes and lights one. It's long and skinny with a pastel band where the filter starts. She can't say anything, I guess, with her mouth full of cigarette. So I talk again.

"Did you guys wonder where we went?"

She clips the cigarette between two fingers and holds it away from her face, then leans her head back and blows out a river of smoke. She looks, I don't know, ladyish. Like an olden-days movie star.

"Nope. Didn't even notice you were gone."

"Oh," I say.

I feel really lame all of a sudden, the way I used to feel with Kim when her friends were around. A cigarette'd fix it, but I'm not asking Jo for one of her mom's.

"What'd you guys do?" she asks from behind a curtain of hair. Like every great rocker, Jo wears her hair big, curly, and over her eyes. Most of the time I love that we don't make eye contact, but this weekend it's making me nervous. There's something she's not saying. If I can't see her eyes, I won't know what it is.

"Well, we went to his house, and we fooled around. A lot, I mean."

She takes a drag so hard her cheeks go hollow; then she stabs her cigarette out in the brown metal ashtray.

"Oh yeah?" she says, torquing up another. "How'd that go?"

I think of the house's smallness, and Steve's boniness. Of how fun it should've been, and how scary it actually was. Of the silence between us when we walked back to the Zarzozas'. I try to think how to explain all of that to her. It doesn't work.

"It was okay. Can I get a drag of that?"

Joanna tosses me the pack, which means I'm gonna steal from Mrs. Azore. I light it with a prayer she stays in bed or wherever she is, 'cause I really don't like stealing from people who are nice to me. Joanna stares at the TV.

"Yeah, so, Jo?" I say. "He, like, asked if I wanted to do it."

Joanna's the queen of cool. I could be telling her I lost my virginity last night, but all she does is finish her drag, turn her head, and raise her right eyebrow at me. That's it. She doesn't even say anything.

So I do my thing. I sweat and stutter and stutter and sweat. "Are you crazy? No fucking *way*! But Jo. I was, like, terrified. I mean, we came so close—we were alone in his house, and he, like, had his hand in my pants, and what was I gonna say? Just, *No*!?"

She stares at me. Her mouth stays in a straight line, except when she puckers to put her cigarette to her lips. Then she raises her other eyebrow. That eyebrow says plenty.

"So I didn't say *no*, exactly. I pretty much said not *yet*. But I'm freaking out. I mean, if I don't, would I even be allowed at Zarzozas'? Should I have said yes? What would I do when we're in Bridgeport if he doesn't like me anymore?"

For a sec, Jo hooks my gaze with hers. There's a lot happening in her mind, but I can't figure out quite what. Then she turns back to the TV. She smokes slowly. I smoke fast.

On Sunday, we don't talk about Saturday night. We don't talk about how Steve didn't ask if I wanted to leave the Zarzozas' and go back to his house, or how Rich was there and how he said, really loud, "Hey Jo! It's your turn to come back to the water bed! Eh. I just looked at ya. Never mind."

We don't talk about how everybody laughed at that, even her, but not me. Instead, we talk about Kara Anderson.

Kara Anderson is this weasel chick who's on the fringes at our school. She's not a jock. She's not exactly a loser, and she's no *way* a hood like us, even though she wants to be. She's not cool enough for Levi's, but someone got her some work boots, which she wears all laced-up and tied. Fuckin', duh! She hangs out at the edge of the smoking pit, trying to make people like her by talking shit about the cool kids.

Last week, the person she talked shit about was Joanna. Probably Kara thinks it's safe to talk about Jo 'cause Jo only just moved to Monroe. Probably she thinks people don't know Jo yet, so she can say whatever she wants. What she doesn't know is that Jo's my best friend, and that when I'm pissed, I turn into the Hulk. Kara is a stupid, stupid girl.

So Sunday morning, when we're back in front of the TV, Jo tells me what's up. "Check this out," she says. "Kara Anderson's telling people her cousin went to junior high with me." There are no cigarettes on the table today, so Jo's chewing a big purple wad of gum instead. "She's saying her cousin said I'm a whore."

Jo doesn't seem mad. So I get mad for her. "Are you fucking kidding me? You're not a whore!"

"Right? I *wish.* So pretty much, Kara's trying to look good by making me look bad. What a winner, huh?"

I don't know why Joanna's laughing at this, but I'm not. I'm on fire. And through the flames, I see some kind of a chance. I can't really explain it, but Kara Anderson's gonna get me past that wall in Jo's eyes.

"I'm gonna get 'er, Jo," I say, "Watch. I'm gonna kick her ass. *Fuck* her."

Joanna tongues the gum blob to the front of her teeth and holds it there for a second, half-in and half-out of her mouth. She looks at me; then she shrugs. "'Kay," she says and goes back to chewing. She blows a big, hazy bubble, and I smile.

In his zip-up work jumper, Mr. Azore looks more like Mario than ever. Even at 7:28 on Monday morning, he's smiling. But his smile falls a notch when Jo kicks the car door open in front of the school. "What? No kiss?" he says.

"Bye, Dad."

Joanna has no fucking idea what she's got.

It's 7:29 when we step out of the car, which means we have to book it to first period and pray we're not marked tardy. Jo's work boots flop as she runs down the hallway, throwing another "bye" over her shoulder at me. The last thing I see are her Sammy Hagar curls, swinging against the hood of her sweatshirt.

A stripe of loneliness cuts through me as the 7:30 bell rings, then ricochets down the empty hallway. Petting Mr. Azore's T-shirt hem, I make my way to Spanish class.

I haven't been in Spanish five minutes when a knock pulls

all eyes to the door. The knocker opens the door without waiting for a *come in.* A woman scans the class while faking an apology. That's when I put my head down.

"I'm sorry to interrupt, Mrs. Rosenstein, but I have a bit of an emergency with a parent." The bad vibe officially kicks in. "Do you have a Cynthia Etler in this class?"

I knew it. I shoulda hid in the Azores' attic in Bridgeport.

As if she's in shock from being interrupted, Señora Rosenstein says nothing for a sec. Then she goes, "Yes, yes I do. Cynthia…Etler, where did I put you? I just rearranged my seating chart…"

My forehead is on my desk, so I can't see these two bitties, but I can feel them scanning the seats with their laser-beams. Still, I don't budge. No way am I volunteering for this shit.

"Cynthia Etler? Cynthia, where are you?"

Somebody kicks the leg of my chair, undoubtedly the asshole jock behind me. I don't think school employees kick students, usually. Still, I better say something. It's not like they're not gonna find me.

"Yeah," I heave out as I stand. "I'm with ya."

Everyone stares at me as I move toward the door. Someday, I swear, I'm gonna live where nobody can see me.

It turns out the lady at the door is my guidance counselor. She's got her hair in the Connecticut bob, like she wants to be all Fairfield County. But her clothes are totally Dress Barn. If she's nice to me, I'll feel sorry for her.

"So, you're Cynthia?" She's smiling as her heels click

down the hallway, but I don't answer. "I'm Ms. Grass. If you struggle in your classes, or your peer relationships become challenging, I'm here for you."

I study the tiny diamond in her earlobe. It's smaller than your average pencil point. Yeah, I feel bad for her. She's trying pretty hard.

She chatters the whole way to her office, but when we step inside, she gets serious. She gestures toward a chair, then turns on a little machine. A swishing noise kicks in, I guess to cover our "talk" from eavesdroppers. As if I'm going to be sharing heavy secrets with this lady. I feel extra bad for her now.

"So, Cynthia," she says. "What's going on with you?"

She must not remember the hot pink WHILE YOU WERE OUT slip that's front and center on her desk. She already knows what's going on with me, or at least what my mother says is going on.

> Nadine Etler, parent of Cynthia Etler-
> VERY CONCERNED-Student gone since
> Thursday. Mother TERRIFIED. Use
> caution! Student may be volatile!

Awesome. Volatile. We learned that word in eighth grade vocab: it means crazy violent. To my mother, I'm the volatile one. But I gotta hand it to Ms. Grass. She's doing good for someone alone in a room with a crazy, violent teenager.

There's nothing to say, so I say nothing. But it's okay. Ms. Grass is the type who doesn't mind doing the talking.

"Your mother called the school, Cynthia. She's looking for you. She's very concerned that you weren't home over the weekend. I haven't spoken with her personally, but I assume it's a simple mix-up—confusion about which friend you were spending the weekend with?"

"Oh, yeah. Totally. She's just confused. My neighbor should've reminded her I was staying at their house. I'll call her from the pay phone." I even sort of smile.

"Well good then, Cynthia!" She brings her hands together in a clap. "You may use my phone, if you'd like."

"Nah, that's okay. I don't want to take up your office. I've got a dime. I'll call her at lunch. Thanks, though."

"Well, Cynthia, you're most welcome. Really, I have no idea why anyone would say—well, you're a thoughtful young lady. Let me write you a pass back to class."

I have the smoking pit to myself for the rest of the period. My mother figured out I wasn't at Dawn's this weekend, and now she's after me. Jo only asked if I could stay with them for the weekend, and the weekend's over. I sit and smoke and try not to let myself think.

I don't see Joanna at lunch, which is weird. Somebody said she had to stay in science for a make-up test, but Jo? No way.

Badasses don't do makeups. My insides feel like a dried-out sponge. Scratchy, holey, and easily snapped in half.

I don't see her at the end of the day, either. Her bus is the first one to leave, and I don't get out front 'til after it's gone. Mrs. Skinner—the one cool teacher, who notices stuff—kept me after class, like, "Are you okay, Cyndy?" At least she knew enough to be writing in her grade book instead of that deep, caring eye contact bullshit. But there's nothing she can do for me. You can't go live with your teacher, so there's no point telling her anything. And her caring only made shit worse, 'cause it made me late for the bus, and now I can't find Jo. So I have no idea where I'm supposed to go tonight.

I'm running along the row of buses, hoping for a miracle, like Joanna's face in the window of a bus that hasn't left yet. Instead, six steps ahead of me, I see tight-ankle work boots and lightning-wash jeans. Skinny ass, limp perm. It's *her.*

You know how sometimes when boys are standing around, picking teams or whatever, and a strong kid will pound the basketball hard, with both hands, down at the pavement? Know how the ball rips back upward, like it wants to kill him? That's what my blood does when I see her: it rips through me like I can do *any*thing, including beat the shit out of Kara Anderson.

"Kara Anderson!" It's the same tone the cheerleaders used when they told the whole cafeteria I had a free lunch card in seventh grade. But I'm even louder. Her perm twirls out around her head as she turns.

"You been talking about Joanna Azore?" My voice sounds like someone else's. But she might not even hear it, 'cause I'm handcuffing her shoulders and shaking her like a baby rattle. And oh my God, does it feel good.

In the back of my brain I hear the slats of bus windows opening, the roar of kids cheering. But that doesn't matter. Nothing does, except this power. This rush. This hate. I throw Kara onto the sidewalk like she's the basketball.

"You don't! Fucking! Talk! About! *Joanna!*"

I'm pulling my fist back to hit her when I see the security guard huffing toward me and some suit-wearing grown-ups right behind him. Time for me to fly.

7

PERMISSIONS MUST BE REQUESTED 72 HOURS IN ADVANCE & BE OKAYED FIRST BY PARENTS, THEN STAFF

It's a long walk to Jo's from school, especially when the walk starts with running from a pack of pissed off adults. Every time I hear a car behind me, my stomach curls like a fist. Is it a cop? Are they after me? I turn to look at cars as they pass, but instead of a blue-hatted cop named Rudy, fleshy little kids stare at me through the windows. What, they've never seen someone hauling ass before? I hate this town. God, gimme Bridgeport.

I had *sprinted* down the Masuk driveway—I mean, there was *smoke* coming out of my footprints. But now, a half-hour up the road, I'm walking regular. My feet match the drums in Zeppelin. "Houses of the Holy." Thank God for my headphones.

I guess normal kids have different people to give them what they need. A mom for hugs and a dad for fun and safety.

They have grandparents for buying them stuff, and cool aunts and uncles to teach them what their parents won't. I don't have that kind of family. My mother is not a Band-Aid giver. And the other relatives I have—Uncle Bob and Aunt Judy, the Etlers from my father's life before me—my mother doesn't like them, or they don't like her or something. I pretty much never see them, so I don't *have* them.

But I'm okay. The way other kids get their needs met from their family, I get what I need from my music. When I put on my headphones, I'm in a world that cares. Like this song, "No Quarter." It's about kids with no homes, with no "quarters" to stay in.

The voice ripples in a way that breaks your heart, and a piano plays sad notes that say, "We get you." It's like you're listening to heaven, and heaven's telling you that everything is gonna work out.

Zeppelin understands kids like me, how no doors open for us. But they also say there's a reason for what's happening. I may not get it yet, but that's okay. 'Cause I have Zeppelin. And Floyd. And the Stones. My headphones are my quarters. So I'm okay.

When I get to Jo's I ring her doorbell. It plays a whole friggin' song when you press it. But when the song ends, I'm still standing there. So I press it again. That's when Mrs.

Azore opens the door. Doorbell music is playing as we both start talking at once.

Ding

Ding

Ding

Dong

"Hey, Mrs. Azore. Is—" / "Cyndy, I just spoke with—"

Ding

Ding

Ding

Dong

"—Joanna here?" / "—your mother. I'm sorry. You can't stay with us anymore."

CLANK.

That's how the song ends, with the brass knocker clanking out the period as the door closes hard.

By the time I get to Dawn's, the sun's going down. Through their back kitchen window, I see the family around the dinner table. They're having macaroni and cheese and hot dogs and milk. My stomach growls, and not just for the food. I sit down on the top step and look at the sunset. I'll knock after they put their dishes in the sink.

Dawn ends up saying I can sleep on the daybed, in their upstairs front hallway. It's parked right under the window that faces the road. If I put my face in that window, I'm looking at my mother's house. I'm not letting my face get anywhere near that window. Windows work in reverse too.

By the time I go to finger-brush my teeth, her kids are asleep. The house is all quiet. But right when I sit down to pee, I hear Dawn and John go into their room and close the door. I wasn't planning on spying on them, really. But as I creak the bathroom door open, I hear my name in a slanty tone. Like, *Cyndy*.

It's John. Straight-up-and-down John. Toyota-driving, never-take-a-day-off-work-John. John who'd love to help me, if he could do it without breaking any rules. Maybe John's never seen real evil. Maybe that's why he doesn't get the deal with Jacque.

"We have to tell them she's here," says John.

"John—" goes Dawn. She understands shit.

"They consider it kidnapping, Dawn. The police are involved. Are you going to call Nadine or should I?"

It's quiet for a minute. I picture all of Dawn's dolls listening to their conversation. I hope, like John, they don't understand bad stuff. A floorboard creaks, then Dawn's voice.

"I'll call her."

Quiet as smoke, I'm back in the front hall, under the scary window. My stomach is a bad science experiment as I try to get my Levi's on without standing up in front of that window. They're scrunched around my ankles when Dawn walks in.

"Packin' up?" she asks, pulling my Jansport toward her.

"Well, yeah. I heard you guys. Sorry. I'm outta here."

Dawn pulls the zipper on my pack back and forth as I lie down and bridge my butt up, then pull my jeans on the rest of the way. When I suck my belly in and start buttoning, Dawn speaks.

"I'm not gonna do it," she says.

I sink the bridge down to see her better.

"Huh?"

"I'm not telling your mother you're here."

She stops zippering. She told her husband she'd do it, but she's not going to. Which means she lied for me.

"Really, Dawn? You won't call her? 'Cause if they find me, I'll be—"

"I'm *not* calling her."

"You *prom*ise?"

I pick my eyes up enough to look at hers, and dag. I've never seen Dawn with mad in her eyes. I hope I never see it again.

"I'm not calling her. But I'm telling John I did."

I should thank her, but that would feel so flimsy. Dawn pushes herself up and gives me this weird hug, where she's standing and I'm on the floor.

"G'nite," she says, with her normal Dawn face back on, before going down the hall to her room.

When they're all asleep, I go out and sit on the back porch. The night smells just like Bridgeport. I guess October smells the same wherever you go.

I can't stay here after tonight. By tomorrow, my mother and Jacque will know where I am. John will call them. So tomorrow night, I'll be wherever. I don't know where wherever is, but I know, at least, what it will smell like.

8

NO HITCHHIKING OR PICKING UP HITCHHIKERS

Tina's drawn to me like Jesus to the pathetic. Something about her fat-girl, frosted-hair, ranch-house life needs to save someone, and here I am. She was nowhere to be found last year, when I ate my lunch in a bathroom stall. But now that I'm a smoking pit hero? Poof! Here she is with an offer to stay at her house. I guess she heard about Jo's parents' shutting me out. I guess everybody has.

When I called Steve from Dawn's Monday night, his dad said I can't stay there either. So my new home was about to be a sleeping bag under a highway bridge. Me, the needles, and the used rubbers. Then Tina comes bouncing up.

"Hey, Cyndy! What's up!"

Like we're great friends or something. I raise an eyebrow at her, 'cause she's only trying to impress the juniors I'm sitting with.

"Hey, anyway, Cyndy," she goes, "I heard you—I mean, I heard Joanna's—hey, if you need a place to stay, my father said it's okay. You can come stay with us."

Us. What a word. Two letters that hold everything I've ever wanted. Some people can throw their "us" around, all casual like that. If I had an "us," I'd carry it in a little satin bag, with both hands cupped around it. But for Tina, it's just a lure. Still, she's offering her "us" to me. That's better than a bedroll and a bridge.

So now, pretty much, I have a new best friend. I've just gotta tell Joanna it's only for show. Jo will always be my real best friend, even though I haven't seen her since she took off down the hallway Monday morning. Where *is* she?

But Joanna or not, I'm a rock star in the pit now. No joke. I get off the bus at school Tuesday morning—after the *creepiness* of walking to the bus stop from Dawn's, praying nobody sees me—and I walk into the pit…and it goes silent. I go down the steps and people—I'm talking hoods here, including seniors—step back and clear a path for me.

"Hey, Cyndy. How you doin'?" someone says.

I keep my eyes straight ahead, 'cause for all I know, they're making fun of me. Except they totally aren't.

One of the big, silent dudes peels himself off the wall, comes over, and puts his hand on my arm.

"How you doin', Etler? Come hang with us."

Next thing I know, I'm sitting in the coolest, scariest spot in the pit, just me and these guys. And I got invited. By name.

Other than being big, these guys are cool because they don't talk. They're like gargoyles, so still you're not even sure they're alive. But one of them moved for me. And another one spoke.

"Hey, heard about your sitch, Etler. That's rough."

So the cool people know my name *and* they're talking about me when I'm not there? Holy crap. I guess homelessness + kicking poser ass = badass.

So I'm sitting there with the gargoyles Tuesday morning when Tina comes up. She looks all teenybopper, even to me. Like the clown on the spring in the jack-in-the-box.

"Hey, Cyndy! What's up!" **Boing! Doi! Boing!**

And it hits me, oh my God, I'm looking down on somebody. Fuckin' A. I'm, like, cool. On the inside. But I should be nice because, thanks to Tina, I get to sleep in a bed tonight. It's tucked in a corner of her basement. What is it with me, beds, and basements? At least at Tina's, somebody hung a sheet so I have privacy.

So staying at Tina's is okay. Her mom is one of those ladies who wears rollers and watches soaps all day, and her dad is—you ready? A hairdresser. No, really. Not a *bar*ber, a *hair*dresser. He does Monroe ladies' hair in a beauty shop.

And Tina's all right, too. Seriously. She talks like the Tasmanian Devil, fast and nonstop, but at least I don't have to figure out what to talk about. And anyway, the only time I have to see her is in the morning and afternoon, when we take the bus. Somehow she picked up on the message to not come in the smoking pit anymore. Chunky, pink-sweatshirt, no-cigarette Tina, talking to me on fast forward? No sir.

On Thursday, after my second night at Tina's, Jo comes up to me. I'm like, *huh*? I mean, she's totally been avoiding me. I don't know if she's pissed I'm staying at Tina's or what, but here she is, heading for my new spot with the gargoyle guys. She pushes her fist toward my hip and goes, "Early birthday present." I slant my eyes from her fist to her face, and she knocks her chin at me.

"Go ahead," she says.

I lay my hand flat, and she uncurls her fist. A blue velvet bag, the weight of a lemon, drops into my open palm.

"Jo. Your pipe?"

"Happy fourteenth, Cynd. Make it a good one."

I want to ask her how. *How* do I make it a good one? But she'd just say, "Smoke up, man!" I'd *so* be a loser if I asked her how to do *that*. But seriously, I still don't know. I'll take, like, one paranoid hit, terrified I did it wrong while everyone watches. Then I act like I'm too stoned for more, and sit there praying bullets some Zarzoza doesn't say what everybody's thinking: "You're such a poser. Get the fuck outta here."

Anyway, speaking of my birthday, I bet you ten bucks that's why I haven't been called back to the guidance office. My mother stopped looking for me because she doesn't want me back. Not yet. If I'm not there on my birthday next week, she won't even have to bake a cake. But October

18? Day after my birthday? I'll be right back in Ms. Grass's office. Watch. My mother will call the school the second it quits being about me, and can switch back to being all about her.

Or maybe not.

I'm on my way to the bus after seventh period when I hear my name.

"Cynthia Etler."

The syllables of my name snap like gunshots, in time with the speaker guy's footsteps.

I try my usual trick. Nine out of ten grown-ups will disappear if you ignore them. But this guy is that fearless one in ten.

"This her?" another voice asks, from *directly* behind me.

I'm about to take off, but they get me by the scruff of the neck. Right there in the Masuk High School entrance. Everybody's watching as I do the Fred Flintstone, scrambling my legs in the air.

Whoever this guy is, he's fast and I'm powerless. He steers me toward the office, and he's not fucking around. Ms. Grass is suddenly here, pushing the office door open, and even she looks scared. But I shouldn't be *that* surprised. I knew I couldn't skate; I saw this hard end coming. Something, somehow, had to stop me.

So now I'm under arrest. No joke. My mother put out a warrant for me. No, I swear to God. Turns out she made one call to the school—that was when Ms. Grass pulled me into her office—and that was enough of an effort for her. Her next call was to Rudy the youth officer, because I'm "out of control." Next stop: Monroe Police Department.

At the precinct, I get my fingertips stained by a cop. He's, like, manhandling me, gripping each finger and rolling it across an inky pad. The harder he presses my finger, the more juice floods the pad.

As my fingertips are drying, the cop brings me to a room made of glass. Waiting for me there is Rudy, the "youth officer." I bet Bridgeport has, just, *officers*, you know? Sitting across from two big police guys, the memory of getting handcuffed in front of the school still fresh, I feel like the fly in the spider's web. Why can't I move? Why aren't my wings working? What's that *thing* coming at me?! Fuck!

The Cyndy who knocked Kara Anderson down in front of the buses is *gone*. I fold my arms across my boobs to get my toughness back, but the cop says, "Put your arms down." It's not a request. He's got a gun.

I've never heard anything quieter than this room. There's not even a ticking clock to think about. I stare at the table and wonder what I'm supposed to be doing. Finally, Rudy's Styrofoam cup squeaks on the tabletop. I hear the **clunk** of his swallow. Then he speaks.

"Cynthia."

My eyes are dried out from staring at the table. I could use a blink. Still. I just stare. I don't speak.

"Cynthia," he says again. He sounds like he could "Cynthia" all day.

Okay. Uncle.

"Yeah?" I say, and let myself have one, wet, blink.

"Cynthia."

I've gotta look at him too? Okay, I'll do my trick. When Jacque plays the "Lookit me when I talk to you" game, I lift my eyes to his drunkflush cheeks, but never to his actual eyes. That way he's not winning, but he thinks he is.

My trick works on Rudy too.

"Your mother is here."

My heart cracks in half. I'm gonna get hauled back to that house. She gets to just hand me back to her husband. And I have no say.

"You have a choice to make."

"I do?"

"You can go home with your mother—"

Choice Two must be *bad*, because everything in the room turns dark. Rudy's face, the lights, the mood. His voice sounds like judgment day.

"—or you can go into foster care."

POOM! Choice Two is a torpedo. My cracked heart explodes into fireworks.

I'm the kid who got a pony for her birthday. My face is too small to hold my grin.

"Foster care! Thank you!"

See? I told you. God's giving me a do-over! This time

I'm gonna get a family straight out of a Judy Blume book, with a mom who wants to know how my day was, and a dad who ruffles my hair. If the smoking pit could see me now, bouncing up and hugging a cop? I'd be banned for life.

9

NO MAKING OR RECEIVING PHONE CALLS OR LETTERS

Thank God it's not a tart cart that drives me away from the police station—a short bus would have ripped the thrill right out of this. Instead, it's one of those blue vans, with the backseat windows that pop out at the bottom. I don't know how such a tiny lady can drive this thing. The steering wheel's as big as the moon.

This lady, she looked *so* out of place in the police station. She was the only one there not beige or cream or white. But she didn't care. You could tell by the way she walked. She made quick steps in her high heels that undid the official silence. She's done this before. She's my hero.

After I hugged Rudy—yeah, I really hugged him—he brought me to the waiting room, which was the size and temperature of a refrigerator. There was a woman there waiting for me who looked familiar, like your favorite baby toy showing up in the basement. Like, *Oh man, I kind of remember this!*

The woman was my mother. I didn't say anything to her. I wasn't trying to be mean. I just didn't feel like I knew her well enough to say hi.

"Mrs. Etler, Cynthia has made her decision," Rudy said.

Then he looked at me like I was supposed to do the talking.

"Can you tell her, please?" I mumbled to my Keds.

Rudy didn't mumble back. His words were loud and clear. "It's your decision. You need to tell her yourself."

This is why people hate cops, right? But then the other cop brought the high-heeled lady in, and somehow, she gave me strength. I looked at her, this stranger with black skin and kind eyes, and I told her my decision. I said it to the lady.

"I'm going to foster care."

Magically, this lady knew what I needed. With two clicks, she was standing in front of my mother, blocking her from seeing me. She put her hand out to shake.

"Neekka Smith, Janus House Youth in Crisis." Her voice belonged to a queen. "I'll be taking Cynthia to Janus House now."

She turned to the cops. She looked them in the eyes, no problem. "Thank you, Officers."

Then she turned and high-heeled it out of the room. I Ked-scuffed out behind her, as if it was just that easy, all along.

Neekka and the van took me to Janus House, which is...in *Bridgeport*! God, I'll never doubt you again. God *damn!* I'm living in Bridgeport, *and* I'm away from Jacque. My life couldn't be any better.

Neekka's one of the four staff here. She's still my hero, but she's not my favorite. She's a little strict. All the staff makes us follow the same rules, but some of them are cooler with how they do it.

Pretty much, the staff lets you decide for yourself how it's gonna go. They're all, "Here're the rules. It's up to you if you follow them or not." So if you choose to follow the rules, you get privileges. If you choose to *not* follow them, you get consequences. It's all the same to staff, either way. Crazy, right?

My first night here, they tell me I have "kitchen clean-up" as a chore. And I act how I would at my mother's house. I sit there with a plate of "food" in front of me and I go, "No way. I didn't eat, so I'm not cleaning." You know, loud. And then I don't move.

Staff goes, "Okay. You guys have until six thirty to do your chores. If you're not done by then, you lose evening privileges. If you still haven't done them by seven o'clock, you lose the next day's afternoon privileges too. It's up to you."

That's it. Totally calm too. There's no yelling, no threats. Just the facts and my choices.

At seven thirty-five that night I was sitting upstairs, pulling threads out of my bedspread with fingertips all pruney from dishwater. Let me tell you something. Sitting alone, listening to all the other kids in the TV room, makes you realize how much you really *want* to do your chores.

You can't get away with jack shit at Janus House, but it's worth it. Because no matter what you do or don't do here, you're *safe*. It's like Disney World. I'd only been here a week on my birthday, but they still made me a cake, and sang to me, and let me choose what we'd watch on TV. When I went outside for a cigarette, to see the stars and thank God for everything, it hit me why this birthday was so good: because I knew, all day long, that I wouldn't end up trapped in a corner by Jacque some time before bed.

Even the rules are okay, because they might suck, but they also do something good for you. Like, no overnight privileges. Because of that rule, I can't see Steve. Which sucks. He lives out by Father Panik Village, and none of those guys are gonna come pick me up for a day pass. Jo's parents won't either. They've pretty much disowned me since my mother called them. And, like, staff is gonna drive me over my boyfriend's house, so I can smoke pot and get my boobs squeezed? Stop dreaming.

Actually, I did ask Neekka once. "No individual van rides," she said.

The last time I saw Steve was the weekend he asked me to do it, so it's been a few weeks. But that's okay, because we talk every time I have phone privileges. And since I have no way of getting to his house, he has no way of asking me to do it. So no overnight privileges sucks in one way, but it's good in another.

What was *really* good was the first time I got store privileges. Me and this other girl walked to the deli for candy and cigarettes. It felt just like when I lived in Stamford: freedom, with change in my pocket.

Three old men sat in metal chairs out front; somebody's abandoned cigarette sat on the counter, with smoke weaving up like a cobra from a basket. Man, did I feel grown-up. On the walk back to Janus, I packed my Marlboros on the bone of my palm and decided that when I get older, I'm gonna do this for kids like me. I'm gonna help the fuckups and show them how to act. Just like the Janus House staff.

I'm telling you, I could stay at Janus forever. The van drops me off at Masuk every day, so I get to hang out with Joanna and the smoking pit guys. Then I'm free for the whole day, 'cause there's no staff around to check if I'm following the rules. I could be smoking pot in the woods for seven straight hours, and how would they know? Not that I'd know *how,* but I could. And that's what matters.

Just in case I ever get the chance, I carry Joanna's pipe in my denim's front pocket. It's a perfect way to show people how cool I am. Any time someone mentions smoking out, I'm like, "You got some? 'Cause I got a bowl right here," and I slide it outta my pocket. I never have any takers, so I never smoke pot at school. But I totally could.

Nights and weekends at Janus we watch TV and smoke

cigarettes, all of us kids plus whichever staff is on duty. It's perfect. It's a home. I don't even care what staff puts on TV 'cause I'm in this safe place where nobody's fucking with me. They give a shit, but they don't *give* a shit, you know? Only problem is, Janus House is only supposed to let kids stay for thirty days. And I've been here for, like, forty. But they haven't found my foster family yet.

I'm sitting there thinking about all this, about saying thank you to the staff, when Neekka walks in the TV room.

"Come on, Cyndy. Come with me."

I follow her into the staff room. When I walk through that door, it's like I'm walking through a spider web. I feel weird all over my skin, but I can't tell what it is or how to get it off me.

Frank, this staff who swears all the time, is sitting in there. He talks first. He goes, "Cyndy, did ya wanna siddown?"

That's creepy to begin with, because it's a question, not a command. It's not "Siddown, Cyndy," or "Grab a seat, kid," the way he usually talks.

"We got some news for ya."

Is it normal that my belly just dropped, like it went down a hill in a fast car?

I guess Frank doesn't notice my I'm-about-to-barf face, because he keeps going. "Your mother found a place for you."

"My *mother*? But—"

"Hey. Hey, I know. Don't worry, you're not goin' back with your mother. She found a different place for you."

"But I wanna stay *here*! I love it here!"

I've gotten so friggin' soft, there's tears snagging at my throat.

Frank's not saying anything. He pulls on the soft white threads around his jeans' knee holes. Neekka takes over.

"We know, Cyndy. We wish you could stay too. But we only have thirty-days-per-child capacity."

"Is the place a foster home?" I ask in a weeble-wobble voice. Good thing I don't care what staff thinks of me. Staff that's not saying anything. Staff that won't even look at me. "Guys? Is it a foster home?"

What happens next is like a laser light show. Neekka zips her eyes away from me as Frank looks up from his knees. Their looks clap together in the middle, electric, and they say something to each other without words. What the *fuck*?

"It's a—a boarding school, kiddo. In Virginia. Somebody named 'Shirley' found it—your aunt or something?"

"She's my half-sister from my father's—what kind of a boarding school?"

"It's a place like here, a place for asshole kids," says Frank, "Nah, just joshin'. Is that half a laugh? You'll be all right. And you'll come back and visit us, right?"

Way to pat my back in the middle of a beating. But still. "Yeah, Frank. I will."

"So, Cyndy," Neekka says, all business again. "We need you to go upstairs and get your stuff packed. Your mother's coming for you at seven tomorrow morning."

Tomorrow. So I've got no chance to say good-bye to anyone. But other than Joanna and Dawn and Steve, who would I say bye to? I'll see Jo in a few weeks anyway because I'll be back for Christmas break. I'll stay at her house, probably, and I'll have something interesting to talk about for a change: my boarding school for fuckups.

Man, I'll be surrounded by friends at a place like that. We'll lie in the grass under giant old trees and read *No One Here Gets Out Alive* for English class, 'cause our teachers will be old hippies. And I'll have my own room with a window seat. I've read about boarding schools in books, and the bedrooms always have window seats. I'll have Janis Joplin posters on my walls, and we'll make tie-dyes in the girls' room sinks. And I'll finally learn how to smoke pot right! Some cool teacher will probably show me how. When I come back for Christmas, I'll be able to *roll* a joint. If only we could skip over the mother-driving-me-there part. But whatever. It'll totally be worth it to get to my new school.

That weird feeling comes back when I call Steve. But this time, instead of spider-webby, I feel all icy inside. Frank gave me permission to use the staff office phone instead of the pay phone, so there aren't a million people listening. Maybe that's why I'm feeling funky. Like, using the staff phone to call your boyfriend? That's the forbidden dream. So why are they letting me do it?

"Hey, Steve," I go.

"Hey," he says back.

"It's Cyndy."

"Yeah, I know. Sup?"

"Well I don't know, exactly. Something's happening."

"Yeah?"

You'd think being alone in this room, without staff, I'd be digging through cabinets to find out what they really think of me. But I'm so locked in my iceberg, I don't even care.

"Yeah," I say. "My mom's resurfaced. Friggin' Loch Ness Monster. She's taking me to some boarding school."

"Yeah? No shit."

"Yeah."

Neither of us knows what to say next. I want to ask him what the school will be like, but duh, like he has any idea. I also want to tell him how sketchy the staff is acting, but I don't know how to explain it. So we do what we always end up doing: not talking, and listening to the music he's got on. It's Floyd again, *The Wall*. It's that part where marching drums lead into a chorus singing, like, some Nazi hymn. Then it's just one voice holding out one long note, and you can tell the guy is crying, even though he's singing. Then he stops, and somebody's knocking and yelling, "Time to go!" And the people are laughing, laughing.

The Wall's trying to tell me something, but I'm not getting it.

Finally, I think of something to say. "But nothing's gonna change. Actually, it'll be better. I'll call you every night, and I'll be able to stay with you for vacations."

The voice I hear next isn't Steve's. It's coming from the background of his house. "Got Hosebag on the line, there?"

Then it's Steve again. "Listen, I gotta go. I'll talk to ya later, 'kay?"

I'm afraid to hang up. This phone call feels like a tightrope. If it's cut, I'll fall and fall and fall. But what else am I gonna say?

"'Kay. Love you. Bye," I say, but he's already gone.

10

NO TELLING YOUR PARENTS YOUR HOST-PARENTS' NAME OR PHONE NUMBER

When Jacque pulls up in front of Janus House, I feel like slapping someone. Possibly God. I climb into the back-back seat and lie down without a word to my mother or Jacque, like, "I don't see you people." I don't even sit up to wave bye to Neekka and Frank.

Ten silent, awkward hours later, we get to Shirley's house. Once we get there, though, it's like the sun came out. They have real ranch dressing at Shirley's, from a bottle with a label. It's right out on the table, and you can pour as much as you want on your white-lettuce salad. And the chicken is Shake 'n Baked. And Shirley made me a cake, even though my birthday was a month and two days ago. I would give *anything* to live here.

When we sit down for dinner, everyone sings happy birthday to me, and Julie, my older-than-me niece, gives me a real Hallmark card. Inside it says, "Happy 14th!! We love you," and then they signed their names. They *love* me? If they love me, maybe all those times when Kim got to come down here, I could've come too? No *way*. Do over.

But wait. Just 'cause they wrote "I love you" doesn't mean they actually *do*. They're never this nice, not to me. They're just extra nice tonight, for some reason. Everyone keeps using my name, like, "Cyndy, would you like more mashed potatoes?" and "You look really skinny, Cyndy. I'm so jealous!" It's making me feel funny, which doesn't make sense. I'm getting what I always wanted. These people from my father's first family like me back. But why now? What's there to like about me all of a sudden?

It's hard to tell what's actually going on, because Shirley's really good at talking about nothing. Ever since we got here, it's been nonstop happy talk. *Good Morning America*, Julie's new college, Shirley's sewing projects… At my mother's house, everything depends on where Jacque is and what mood he's in. But here, it's like Jacque and Bill, Shirley's husband, don't even exist. They're not talked about, and they're not talked to. How does Shirley *do* that?

However she does it, she's also avoiding the one thing I need to talk about: my new boarding school. It's supposedly really close by, but this isn't the kind of town that has grassy hills and houses with window seats, like I imagined. So what *is* this school gonna be like?

I want dirt, but they're only giving me one nugget, which

you're not going to believe. Shirley heard about my new school on the news, because Princess friggin' *Diana* visited it last week. And Nancy Reagan too. Like, the president's wife! So I mean, even if it's not huge trees and brick and ivy, this school must be pretty nice, right?

"Caaay—ake! Who's ready for some cake?" Shirley sings, as Julie pushes her chair back and starts picking up dishes.

"So what's the name of this joint?" I ask Shirley, whose head is in the fridge. For a minute, it's like she doesn't even hear me. Julie turns the sink on full blast.

"Shirley, what's the name of my new sch—"

Her head's still in the dark of the fridge. But I swear I hear her right when she goes, "Straight."

Straight? Like…as an arrow? Like a long, thin, flying knife?

Shirley lifts the cake out and closes the fridge. She moves to the butcher block and pulls out a long, thin, sharp-looking knife. I don't ask any more questions.

The drive from Shirley's to my new boarding school is short, like ten minutes. We cross over this psycho highway, cars whipping past like they've been flung from slingshots. Then we turn and stop in front of a yellowish brick building. It's all right angles, no windows. I flash back to the feeling I got listening to *The Wall* with Steve the other night, and something tells me to run. But to where? To who? Instead,

I follow my mother and Jacque through the smoked-glass front doors.

Once we're inside I do the fuck-you pose: arms across boobs, bangs over eyes. I'm scanning the place, not missing a beat, when this dork of a guy walks up. He's got a tucked-in collared shirt and dark blue *slacks* on. Did he comb and part his hair with *water*? He's wearing a badge:

What the fuck is a runner?

Okay. I've got a few puzzle pieces here, but the edges don't match up.

Piece #1: I'm going to this boarding school for cool, tough kids like me.

Piece #2: No *way* is this place a boarding school for hoods. I don't know what it is, but it doesn't look good.

Something is *up*. Like, why was Shirley so nervous this morning? Why is my mother so happy? And why is this kid, who's creepily standing next to me now, wearing a badge, not a tie-dyed shirt?

Behind the counter are two more teen robots. Muzak is playing in the background. The girl robot says, "Can I help you?"

My mother steps up. "Yes, you can. We have an appointment." She gives the girl my name.

I look back toward the doors, but two more slacks-wearers are blocking them. Arms folded, legs spread. Man, what the fuck?

Meanwhile, the teenbots behind the counter have sprung into action. It's a well-oiled machine. Counter Girl looks at Runner.

"Cyndy Etler. 8:00 a.m."

Runner turns and marches through a door that, in a flash, is opened from the other side by a paisley-bloused black woman. She *so* doesn't belong at my boarding school. This is no dungareed hippie man; this is a panty-hosed lipstick lady. And her attitude is sharp, totally without that *Welcome, child!* feeling I've gotten from other black ladies.

"Good morning," she says. She doesn't smile. "Mom, Dad, welcome to Straight. One of my colleagues will be with you in a moment. Cyndy. This way, please?" It's a question, but there's no question in her voice.

The sign on her door says "Mrs. Harper—Executive Staff." They must have something against windows at this school, because there isn't even one in Mrs. Harper's office. She points me to a chair that's backed into a corner between her desk and the concrete walls. I'm cornered by the lipstick lady. Yeah, things are really looking up for me at my fun new school.

Mrs. Harper takes her time. She's not good at small talk

like Shirley. The only sound is the **fwisk** of shuffling pages. Finally, Mrs. Harper cracks the ice.

"What drugs have you done?" she asks in a voice made of bullets.

"Wh-what? None!"

I'm trying to talk the way I would to my mother, like, *I don't fucking care*. But I can hear myself. It's not working.

"Are you sure about that?"

She's looking at me, hard.

"*What*? Yeah, I'm sure! I think I'd know if I'd—"

She turns to her desk and opens a drawer. Then she swivels back and opens her fist in front of me. "What's this, Cyndy?"

Her palm looks like puffy pink trampolines. Brown lines, same color as her face, separate one puff from the next. In the middle of her palm there's a little drawstring bag. It's dark blue velvet.

I thought I knew how to say fuck you, but Shirley and Julie? They know the *real* way to do it. I gave Julie that bag last night. I asked her to hold it for me, because *The Wall* was telling me to watch out. Julie promised she wouldn't tell anybody, and I thought trusting her would make us close. But Julie gave it to Shirley. And Shirley gave it to this place.

"That's not mine!" I say. "I don't smoke pot. That's my best friend's."

Mrs. Harper smiles, calm as a crocodile.

"How do you know what's in this bag, Cyndy, if it's not

yours? And if you don't do drugs, how do you know what this device is used for?"

I fall back in the chair, **thunk**. It knocks the wind out of me. Mrs. Harper puts my velvet bag back in her drawer, picks up a clipboard, and writes. You can't see the handcuffs, but they're on me.

"Have you done alcohol?"

Have I *done* alcohol? "No! I haven't. Really!"

"Okay. That's good."

She writes.

"Cyndy, do you attend a church?" She's got a nice smile on her face now. She likes church. Church is my escape hatch.

"I do! I go to Christ Church in Norwalk, and I'm baptized and everything! And then, when we moved, I switched to Monroe Congregational. They're really nice there. You should go!"

"Maybe I'll do that, Cyndy. Do they offer communion with grape juice at Monroe Congregational?"

I've got to show her how into church I am. Okay, details.

"Oh yeah, they do. But I'm old enough to sip from the cup like the grown-ups now. The grape juice is for the little kids."

"Oh, I see. I remember becoming old enough to sip wine from the Blood of Christ cup, and feeling very close to God at that time. Did you feel that way?"

"I did too! Getting to sip wine like the grown-ups made

me feel, like, proud. I walked really tall back to my pew that day."

"That day? Do you still go to church?" she asks.

"Oh yeah! Like every Sunday."

"And of course, you take communion every time you're there."

"Yeahhh..."

She looks at me for a second. Her eyes are the arrow; my face is a bull's-eye. Her smile is gone.

"You told me you don't do alcohol, Cyndy. But you *do* drink alcohol. Every weekend. You lied to me."

When kids fall down well holes—deep, fast, helpless—this is how they feel. They feel *fucked.*

From the well-bottom, I yell, "*What*? But I—"

"What else have you lied about, Cyndy? You've done marijuana and you've done alcohol. What other drugs have you done?"

I'm out of words. I'm out of everything. There's a long silence, then the sound of paper rustling. Mrs. Harper speaks again when she wants to. "How are things with your family, Cyndy? Do you have a good relationship with your father?"

A sound comes out of me, a voice choked with well-sludge. "My father's dead."

"Your father is not dead, Cyndy. He arrived here with you and your mother."

That brings my fire back. *Don't you fucking dare.*

"*That* is not my father. That is my mother's husband. My father died when I was one."

She snaps back with just as much heat. "Your *father* is the man who *raises* you. Therefore, Cyndy, the man who brought you here is indeed your father. Now, I will repeat my question. How is your relationship with your father?"

I'm not here, not in this body, not in this chair. I'm at Janus House, in my scratchy bed. I'm sleeping through this nightmare.

"If you don't talk, you are forcing me to come to my own conclusions, Cyndy. You must not have a good relationship with your father, because you left your father's house to live with your druggie friends. In fact, it seems that you are not sharing a positive relationship with anyone in your family. Am I correct?"

I'm not here. So not here.

"It is my understanding that you are involved in physical violence in your home. Violent behavior is one of the first indicators of drug abuse, Cyndy. Do you realize that?"

I'm not spinning. I'm not trapped.

"I'd like to tell you what I see when I look at you, Cyndy. I see a violent, manipulative young girl, a girl who will do anything to get what she wants, including sleeping anywhere, and undoubtedly with anyone, to obtain drugs. You are lucky to have a mother and father who care enough to get you the help you need. If you are luckier still, perhaps they will allow you to re-enter their home, once you have reformed yourself."

I'm dead, drowned, silent. She picks up her phone and speaks into it.

"Intake three. Send the parents to my office."

Mrs. Harper stands and pushes her chair back, and a flicker of life springs through me. There's a clear path from my seat to the door!

The door opens, and Jacque is standing there.

The flicker goes flat.

"Come in," says Mrs. Harper.

Her face is different now. It's soft and creased with caring. She reaches her palm out for Jacque's hand, then my mother's. She holds their hands for longer than a moment.

My mother's and Jacque's seats are across from her desk. Mrs. Harper turns her chair to them, her back to me. I'm not a part of this conversation.

"Dad, Mom, I've had an informative conversation with Cyndy. As you know, she had been in possession of drug paraphernalia. She also admitted to drinking alcohol, though at first she tried to lie about it. We discussed Cyndy's violent tendencies, and how these are a clear indication of drug abuse. Clearly, she is struggling with addiction."

"What?!" I semi-yell. "But I haven't *done* anything! She's—"

Mrs. Harper's voice slams me back in my seat.

"*That*, Cyndy, is how you will no longer be speaking to your parents. Those days are *over*. Am I clear?"

I look to my mother, begging her with my eyes. Just like

that night in the bathroom. What I see on her face gives me chills. She's glowing like a kid meeting Santa.

My heart just got hit by a truck.

Mrs. Harper keeps going.

"What you're seeing from your daughter, this violent outburst, is called denial. A non-addicted young person would not defend herself with such intensity, and she certainly would not speak to her parents that way. Have you seen this behavior at home, as well?"

Santa just gave my mother her dream toy.

"Yes! I haven't known what to do!" My mother starts crying. "It's been just awful! Cyndy dominates the house with her anger! Anything might set her off, and she'll start screaming, stomping, slamming doors! We're all terrified of her! And I—I haven't known what to *do* about it, how to *help* her. I've tried! But everything I try with Cyndy backfires. She turns angry and—and abusive, toward me, toward the family. I hope you can help my daughter! Can you help my daughter?"

The sobs are gushing out of her. They ricochet off the walls and find me, hunched as small as I can get, in my corner chair. They needle into my skin. Mrs. Harper holds out some tissues to my mother, who stops crying long enough to study the box. *Kleenex Brand*, it says. She takes tissue after tissue after tissue.

Finally, Mrs. Harper turns to me. "Cyndy, what do you have to say for yourself?"

She expects me to cry, to give apologies and promises. But I can't, because the dead don't speak. Mrs. Harper gives me a hate-look. Then she leans forward and picks up my mother's hand.

"She's in more trouble than we knew, Mom. She's lost touch with her emotions. But you've found the right place."

11

NO WEARING JEWELRY OR MAKEUP

The two girls who arrive at Mrs. Harper's door are even dweebier than the one at the front desk. The girl who does the talking has this inch-long hair that lies flat in shingles all over her head. There's an orange barrette clipped right above her forehead. It looks like a third eyebrow. I'm like, *what*?

The girls walk me down a hallway: me in front, talking girl behind me on the right, the other girl behind me on the left. We get to a door and the talking girl, and the one with the barrette, puts her arm out.

"Stop," she says.

"*What*?" She thinks she can command me?

"Stop here. Open the door."

"What are you *talk*—"

"Open the door, Cyndy."

It's like she didn't hear me, like she's a zombie or something. Fine. I'll open the stupid door. Whatever.

Behind the door is an empty room with beige-beige walls and puke-green cafeteria tiles. The only things in the room are three blue plastic chairs. And now me because the zombies are crowding me in from behind.

"Sit in that chair," the talking girl says.

It's obvious which chair I'm supposed to take: the one that's the front point of the triangle. The other chairs are—one guess? Right in front of the door.

Looking at these chicks, all I can say is, man. I am so glad I'm not one of them. They're wearing old-lady, flowered button downs and brand new, no-name jeans with huge, rolled-up cuffs. And here's the worst: no makeup! Their faces look like pancakes before they're cooked. Being nice, I tell them I can help them.

"You'd look really good if you wore makeup," I say. "I could show you h—"

"We're here to talk about you, Cyndy. Not us."

"God, *fine*. I'm just saying." That's what I get, trying to make friends with the hall monitor. I'll find cool kids in English class, though. No doubt.

"We have a list of questions to help us get to know you better. You need to be totally honest. Okay?"

"Yeah, whatev."

"Okay. Cyndy, do you like music?"

Now this is more like it. Maybe these chicks do have some hidden cool.

"Hell, yeah, I like music! Don't you?"

"What music do you listen to?"

Fuck yeah. I'll talk about music all day. "Oh, I love the Stones. And Zeppelin and Floyd. Those are my favorite groups. Pretty much anything they play on PLR and i95, you know? I used to be into like Mötley Crüe and Def Leppard, but not so much anymore."

"Okay. That's enough. Where do you hang out?"

See? This is fine, man. These loser chicks want to hear about my cool life, so they can learn to be cool too. That Mrs. Harper lady, she's just some old bitty. The kids here, they're all right. This school is gonna be okay. So I tell 'em about Bridgeport and why it's the place to be. And when they ask who I hang out with, I tell them all about Jo and Steve and the Zarzozas. They're just burning with jealousy that I have a twenty-eight-year-old friend named Shithead!

For the next question, it's like this girl's got bionic vision.

"Do you smoke pot when you go to Bridgeport?"

"No, man! No! We just—hang *out*. Walk around, listen to music and stuff."

The silent girl finally says something. It sounds like **hmpf**. The talking girl looks at her, then back at me.

"So you go to this dangerous city to hang out in basements with men twice your age. And you sit around and *talk* to them? What does a fourteen-year-old girl talk about with grown men?"

"Man, I don't know! We just talk! We hang out! What the fuck?"

"So you're telling me you've never smoked pot in Bridgeport."

"No."

"But you know what pot *is*."

"Of course! Everybody knows what pot is!"

"You've *seen* it."

"Well, yeah."

"But you don't *smoke* it?"

"No, I don't smoke it! I mean, I know what it *is*, I've been around when other people smoke it, but *I* don't. I don't like that shit."

With that barrette pulling her bangs back, the girl's got a lot of forehead. That's what I notice as she stares at me. That and her tiny, stumpy eyelashes.

"How do you know you don't like it if you've never smoked it?"

And that's when I lose it. "Man, *fuck* this. I'm going out for a cigarette."

They're on their feet so quick, their chairs screech on the tiles.

"No, you're not."

Both girls are posed like Wonder Woman, legs spread, hands on hips.

"Fuck you, I'm not. Lemme by."

Barrette Chick gets the Hulk power. I see it in her eyes. She's gonna kick the shit outta me.

"You're not leaving, Cyndy. You have been signed into Straight by your parents."

"Fuck *that*!"

I'm shouldering between them when the door is thrown open. Before I know what's happening, two guys, the door losers from the front office, surround me. One's behind me and one's in front, *way* the fuck too close. My-nose-on-his-shirt close. I'm lifting my arms to push him away when something's jammed down the back of my jeans. That's when I start screaming.

"*FUCK Y—*" I get out. Then I'm ripped in half as my jeans are wrenched up my crack. I'm jerked backward so fast that my legs can't keep up. It's my Levi's, slinging into my ass and z-z, that catch me from falling.

I yank around to get out of whatever I'm caught on, and I see two things at once: the hairy hand of a door loser grabbing the back of my jeans, and my mother. Standing here, in this room, seeing this. And not stopping it.

A caramel voice says, "Cyndy, your parents are here to say good-bye."

I'm screaming as *The Wall*'s laughter kicks up in my head. Now I know what they were laughing at: my boarding school visions and my stupid, little-kid trust.

"*YOU CAN'T! DON'T LEAVE ME HERE! MOM! MOMMY! DON'T! WHY ARE YOU DOING THIS? DON'T LEAVE ME, MOMMY!*"

But it's like she doesn't hear me. She doesn't even blink.

I'm twisting around, trying to get my Hulk back, and I'm *almost* there, but I—I can't—rip—*off*—this hand dug into my jeans.

Twisting as I scream, I see the door loser's face. It's calm. And so is Barrette Chick's. And her silent friend's, Mrs. Harper's, and my mother's. And Jacque—he's fucking smiling. They're all calm and happy as they watch me, the crying, screaming cyclone on a leash.

"*MOMMY!*"

I lunge at her, and get sliced up the ass again as I'm jerked back. My tears fling forward and land at my mother's feet.

"Good-bye, Cyndy," she says. Then she walks out of the room.

"Bye, Cinny," Jacque mouths.

Or maybe he says it out loud. I can't hear him through my screams.

12

NO GETTING OUT OF SEAT WITHOUT PERMISSION

The beige room gets even smaller as more people cram in. The door guys alone take up half the space, and two new kids, one guy and one girl, are in here now too. Barrette Chick calls them "staff" when they walk in.

The "staff" guy says they're gonna see if I'm carrying. Then he says, "Drop your pants and underwear. Bend over." So I bend. Do I have a choice?

They're all behind me now, and I can feel them looking at me. My fingers are on my toes and my face, red and slimy, is the size of a beach ball. I've shed tears today that have been in storage for fourteen years.

I don't know if it's the guy or the girl "staff," but I hear the snap of a rubber glove. Two hands peel my butt apart, harder and farther than it wants to get peeled. It hurts, but I won't say ***OW***. Some choice words cut through the swirl in my head.

"Clean?"

"Well, I wouldn't say 'clean,' but drug free."

There's laughter, and another rubber snap.

"Cyndy, your intake's over. Bring her to the group."

Then comes Barrette Chick's voice, but with an edge to it. "Pull up your pants, Cyndy."

I pull my stuff up without a word, like I've been following orders all my life. I'm still buttoning my jeans when a hand scrapes down my back again, and a fist clenches onto my waistband. I throw my arms out to steady myself as I'm dragged toward the door. My top button stays undone.

The fist in my spine pushes me into the hall, where my stupid heart trips itself up again. My little girl fantasy tells me my mother will be standing out here. Arms open, face stained with tears, unable to leave me. Like jackrabbits, my eyes flick to the right, to the left—and nothing. Just a row of closed doors. That crushed dream kills something in me. Something important—something like hope. But the fist in my back doesn't pause. It steers me away from the front office.

So I'm walking down this hallway with a hand in my pants. This ugly chick has her fist gripping my waistband, right above my butt. She's pulling my pants up *into* my butt. And I—I can't *do* anything about it. We saw what happened when I tried to fight. A door opens, and that kid with the badge comes walking toward us. The Runner. I don't even care that he's dweeby, he's still a guy. *God, if you're there, don't let Runner see the hand in my pants.*

At the end of the hall, the silent girl leans on an industrial door, then shoves me into a massive room. And what's happening in that room makes no sense. No sense at all. In front of me is this heaving...*beast* made of hundreds of human bodies. There are rows and rows of blue plastic chairs, each chair connected to the one next to it. There's a kid in every chair, and all the kids' bodies are whipping around—back and forth, up and down—like an epileptic mega-seizure.

Listen to me. This beast? It's...it's *fighting* itself. The top half of it is all arms, waving and bending, snapping toward the ceiling. Hundreds of heads shake and nod, but they're not saying yes or no. They're jerking in every direction, and nodding hard like the devil told 'em, "**NOD**." The bottom half of the beast—the bodies below the armpits—are pogo-stick straight, butts glued to their plastic chairs. The only sound is a thrushy breathing and this weird, fleshy clicking. It's a vision of hell.

I'm pushed across the empty half of the room, toward the rattling mass of people and chairs. All I can see are hundreds of backs, but then a few faces twist around to look. Their piston arms keep pumping over their heads, but their eyes are deep and blank. Their eyes are black holes. These kids—these kids are dead inside.

Barrette Chick jerks me to a stop, two feet behind the last row of chairs. The beast's energy pings all over me like Pop Rocks dumped on a tongue. It's bad, but no kind of bad I've felt before. It's—it's fucking terrifying.

With the fist in my Levi's trapping me in place, I know how the damsel in distress felt, chained to the tracks with a train screaming toward her. Only this isn't a game. And I have no hero coming.

Down the middle of the chairs is an aisle. It's the spine of the beast. At the tip of the spine is the beast's head: two teenagers sitting side by side on barstools. From the right stool, a blond girl smiles at me. It's a hungry smile. From the left, a guy spots me over the bashing sea of heads.

"Stop!" he goes, and the beast falls. Every hand, every arm, every head—they all collapse at once. "Incoming!" he shouts.

The million-headed beast turns its black-hole eyes on me. On the left side are boys; on the right are girls that look like boys. No one's wearing makeup, no one's wearing jewelry. And many—way too many—have those third-eyebrow barrettes.

The barstool kid gives a tiny, frowning nod, and the silent girl is suddenly roaring.

"This is Cyndy! She went to Masuk High School in Connecticut! She says she's done pot and alcohol!"

My jeans are yanked farther up my ass, and the beast makes its voice heard.

"Hi, Cyndy! Love ya, Cyndy!"

The faces turn to the front again, and the arms go back up. And all together, with no prompt that I can see, the beast starts convulsing again.

Barrette Chick's hand steers me around the girl side. At the very front row, she pushes my head down so I'm duck-walking. I'm held from behind, getting whacked by flapping arms.

I watch a girl sitting in a chair at the end of the row. At least, a piece of her is in that chair, the edge of her butt. The rest of her is leaning forward, her arms waving at the girl on the barstool.

Barrette Chick leans in toward the girl. She shoves four fingers down the waist of the girl's jeans, nails sliding against the skin of the girl's back. She pushes her thumb through the middle belt loop, makes a fist around the waistband, and pulls the jeans up in a super-wedgie. And the girl just keeps flinging herself around, eyes locked on the barstool blond. *What?* She doesn't *feel* this? This is no problem?

Next thing you know, the girl's pulled out of her chair by the wedgie. The girl crouches next to me; then I'm swung around and *plunk*. I'm in her seat. The hand pulls out of my pants, and *God*, for a second, I feel free. Then I remember where I am: in the very first seat of this psycho beast, three short steps from the hungry blond smiler. I'm trapped in the bull's-eye of this beast.

What the *fuck*?! I want to jump up, screaming, and run. None of these khaki-wearing pansies could catch me. But those big guys? The ones blocking every door? They could stop me, easy.

Craning my neck around, I see that this room goes on

forever. I'm in the middle of a tile-floor Sahara. Running is not in the plan.

A voice cracks out like punishment.

"Jamie C.!"

The beast falls still and the girl next to me stands. Every eyeball in the room turns to look at her. And me. I slump into my seat to get back at them, wrapping my arms across my chest. I look so comfy, I could be in a La-Z-Boy. Fuck you, beast. You don't scare me.

Except, my butt is scared. It hurts like hell. I can't be sitting on hard plastic right now. But I won't let that "staff" know it hurts. Trying to look as tough as I can, I move my arms and slide my hands under my butt. By raising my thumbs I can lever myself up, get a pocket of air back there.

The standing girl starts talking. "I remember the first time I smoked pot, I was with a bunch of popular kids. I only got to be there because my cousin was visiting from California, and—"

The guy on the barstool cuts her off. "Your *druggie* cousin?" he says. He looks sixteen, but his voice sounds way older.

"Yeah. My druggie cousin. They thought she was a movie star or something, because she's totally pretty. And I really wanted to be cool, so I tried to smoke pot. I didn't like it. I coughed 'til I puked, and then I kept coughing and puking. Little bits of my puke got on the popular kids."

Nobody laughs at that. Nobody. That *choice* line, that could make the whole *basement* crack up, wasted. The girl stands there a second, like she's waiting for the laugh, and then she sits down.

"Love ya, Jamie!" the beast screams in one massive voice.

You know in cartoons, when somebody gets trapped in a giant bell, his eyeballs spin and his eardrums pop out when it gets gonged? That's exactly how I feel, sitting in front of that voice. Who *are* these freaks? Where *am* I?

The flapping arms and heads start back up. I take another look around, but I don't like what I find. Up high on the walls, there's a massive row of signs. They're full of, like, God gibberish. Here's what they say.

THE SEVEN STEPS

1. Admit I am powerless over ____________ and come to believe that a power greater than myself can restore me to sanity.
2. Make a decision to turn my will and my life over to the care of God as I understand Him.
3. Make a searching and fearless moral inventory of myself, daily.
4. Admit to God, myself, and another human being the exact nature of my wrongs, immediately.
5. Make direct amends to such people whenever

possible except when to do so would injure them, myself, or others.

6. Seek through prayer and meditation to improve my conscious contact with God as I understand Him, praying only for knowledge of His will for me and the power to carry that out.
7. Having received the gift of awareness, I will practice these principles in all my daily affairs and carry the message to others.

I have no idea what this means, but it has *shit* to do with me, or the God *I* know. How the fuck am I gonna deal with this 'til Saturday?

Saturday will make three days. Back in that torture room, before the "staff" guy walked out, he said I was here for a three-day evaluation. He said, "If we determine you have a chemical dependency and need the help Straight offers, your program will last a minimum of six months."

So. They're gonna "evaluate" me for three days, and then they'll realize how fucking stupid they are. I obviously don't belong here with these drug zombies. They'll see. I'll just sit here and be invisible for three days, watching the freak show. Then I'll go back to Bridgeport with awesome stories to tell.

13

HANG ON TIGHT TO NEWCOMERS BY THE BELT LOOP

There's been this smell, like a big hot fart, for the last hour. There's also been sounds that aren't the beast—a *pang*, then some voices. They're coming from behind a boarded-up window in the wall; there's light in the crack underneath it. But I can't quite hear what's happening back there over the sound of thrashing arms.

Then the barstool guy goes, "Dinner rap!" and people start to move.

Some kids stand, then walk down their aisle of chairs. Others scooch forward in their seats and stay there. There's an ugly girl walking toward me, and the chick in the next chair, "Jamie C.," goes to the edge of her seat. She spins her knees toward the barstools and leans her face forward, offering her ass to the ugly girl, like a dog in heat. It's *twisted*. The ugly girl does that butt-grab thing. She pulls Jamie up with a thumb through her belt loop and four fingers curled into her waistband. Since Jamie's zipper is now level with my face, I can see her jeans cut into her coochie like a string hammock. A fucking *front* wedgie. And she doesn't say a word!

Man, I am *not* having some big monster slice my jeans into my z-z again. Wherever everyone's going, I'll get there on my own. So I stand. I stand and set off a bomb.

"*Sit down*!" a voice blasts.

To somebody, this is an emergency. I look left to see who it is, and there's Barrette Chick, all bulging eyes and dropped jaw. With her hands on my shoulders, she pushes me down *hard*, like I didn't just have a finger crammed up my butt, in that torture room. Like a blast of fire didn't just shoot up through my middle. Then she's reaching around and grabbing the back of my jeans. She shows me how pissed she is as she hauls me to my feet. I feel her fury, right between my legs. I want to fucking punch her, but something stops me, makes me look up…and I see the blond girl on the barstool, staring at me again. This time she's not smiling.

The words from earlier come back to me: "Cyndy's violent tendencies are a clear indicator of drug abuse… You're here for a three-day evaluation."

When I was still in Stamford, this family of bad boys lived down the street. They would hold a magnifying glass over a trapped ant to make it catch on fire. I tried to save the ant by fighting them, but they would knock me down, laughing. Today, I'm the ant. I have three days to make sure I don't catch fire. I drop my eyes and wiggle a little, trying to loosen the z-z-knife. Barrette Chick wrenches it in deeper.

She directs me with a push of her hand, but otherwise, she's silent. Everybody is. In the silence, there's movement, a complicated arranging of bodies. There's a ton of boys, each with another boy's hand holding the back of their pants, in a line at the now-open window. There's this raggedy flock of girls standing twenty feet behind them.

Three days, man. Three days, I tell myself.

When I get to the window, I see where the fart smell was coming from. It's one of those big, lonely church kitchens with the shelves full of pots, each big enough to boil a kid. Under the window, there's a counter lined with Styrofoam trays. Each tray holds a Dixie cup of water, a white bread bologna sandwich, and this gunk, which must be the fart-smell stuff. I want to study it for a second, figure out what it is, but the fist in my spine tells me otherwise. Barrette Chick is digging her knuckles into me, forcing me forward, and it *hurts*. What does she do, lift weights with those knuckles?

When she drops me back off at my seat, I snatch a look around. These kids are sitting up, ramrod straight, eating this shit with one hand and waving their other at the new kids sitting on the barstools. Fucking *freaks!*

Well it's been a lot of hours since breakfast at Shirley's. So I eat the bread, but not the gunk. I'll show them. I don't eat farts.

14

NO HANGING OUT IN PARKING LOT

It feels like ten years have passed since my mother left me here, but somehow, it's still the same day. The beast is lining up again. A new hand is in my pants, and it belongs to some girl named Sandy. I got matched with her when the staff guy, the one who looked in my asshole, stood up with a clipboard.

"Okay, listen up! Host home changes!"

He starts reeling off names, and people get moving. Then I hear my name.

"Cyndy E. with Sandy G.!"

And this girl comes up and grabs me by the butt.

That's about all I know. I'm going somewhere with someone named Sandy, wearing a coat that's not mine. There's a volcano of jackets on the floor behind the beast. Sandy steers me up to it and pulls a ski jacket from the pile. It's purple and orange and cream, and she holds it in front of my nose.

"Nah, that's—"

That's all I get out, before there's a "Shhhh!" in my ear and another upward yank on my jeans.

Still holding it in my face, she gives the jacket a shake, like, "Shut up and take it." So I slide my arms into its sleeves. I just hope there's no lice in it.

Now Sandy's steering me to the end of the long line and pushing me into the back of the girl in front of me. I mean it, she shoves me *into* the poor chick. My nose cuts through her perm like a shark fin slicing water; her butt is flattening my pubes. Sandy's fist is all steel, so I'm locked into place. Then Sandy kicks my feet in, first one, then the other, so they're perfectly lined up with the pube-crusher's sneakers. Her shoes and mine are like those wooden toy trains, the ones with magnets on the ends that link one train to the next.

Sandy wedges herself up tight in line behind me, and I feel my butt pillow against her. It's gross. She spreads and re-curls her fingers against the skin of my back.

A teen drill sergeant goose-steps along the line bawling out, "Heel to toe. Heel to toe."

When she gets close to us, Sandy pulls my jeans up even tighter; she jams her tits in my back. I'm starting to turn around, to give her a What the *fuck*? look, when fingers force my head straight.

"*Heel* to *toe*."

We all stand there, teetering shoe to shoe. The girls' line makes a ninety-degree turn when it reaches the wall; I'm in the back section, so I can see how long, straight, and not normal this is. We're a centipede of teenagers, one latched onto the next.

We've been standing here an hour, I bet, when the whole line goes still. There's no more coughing, no shifting. Finally, the marching Nazi stops and stands at the front of the line.

This grown lady shows up out of nowhere. She's doesn't like us; you can tell by her dead-worm mouth. As she **click-clicks** her way down the line, I drill my eyes into the permy skull in front of me. I'm terrified, though I don't know exactly of what.

"Goodnight, group!" the lady calls at her final click.

"Goodnight!" the hundreds of mouths yell back.

And the line breaks apart. Just like that, all that work, gone. Chains of twos and threes—of heads, arms, and asses—splinter off the line and start walking toward the door.

The *door*!

God, I want to breathe night air, inhale a cigarette. A cigarette! Without even realizing it, I semi-try to run—but I'm attached to a human leash. A person has a lot of control when her thumb is through your belt loop. I'm dragged to the right and then stopped, so other human tricycles can leave before us. She'll teach me to try to go first! That's totally what this is: a lesson. We wait, and wait, and wait. Finally, when everyone else is gone, I'm steered through the door, down a dark hallway, and out into fresh air. Which would be way more heavenly if I didn't have to share it with Sandy.

We're in a parking lot. There are stars overhead. And

maybe God, too, somewhere. There are dinosaur-sized cars, and no one's talking. The only sound is the skidding of pebbles as we kick them across the pavement. Then there's the **ding-ding-ding** of car doors opening, but no loud *sbap!* of doors slamming, after. We are a dark, quiet secret. But at least I can smell the night air. The fucked-up thing is, we're pretty much in public. There are cars driving past us on the street, and if they looked hard enough, the people in those cars could see this girl's hand on my butt.

I take my eyes off the stars, drop them to my toes. Is my mother still at Shirley's house, a mile and a half away? Where's Joanna right now? What's Dawn doing? They're somewhere, right? Doing something. Normal life.

An old-looking kid, his hands in the backs of two other guys' pants, comes up next to us. His eyes are laser-locked on Sandy, like he's refusing to notice I'm here. *Freeeeak shoooow.*

"Hey, Sand," he goes.

He's gotta be her brother, 'cause they look pretty much like twins. I studied Sandy as she walked toward me inside. She has a round face, blond hair, and cream-colored teeth. Her eyes are small, and there's live acne on her chin. Her brother, who's as lumpy round as she is, has big, fresh zits too. They look like potatoes, Sandy and her brother. These are drug addicts?

Finally, Sandy speaks to me. "You're very lucky. You're my only newcomer tonight." She's pushing me across the parking lot toward a maroon minivan. "Dad, this is Cyndy. She just had her intake today."

"Oh!" the dad says from his generic face. But he's smiling at me. "Glad you're with us, Cyndy!"

Are his spread-eagle arms a cue for me to hug him? Do I have to? Sandy decides for me, plowing me right into him. And actually, the hug feels friggin' good. Actually, I could stay right here. Maybe forever. But um, do you know what I did wrong, Sandy's dad? And how have you forgiven me for it?

"Okay guys, pile into the back of the van," the brother says from behind me.

Sandy pulls me back from the hug, and I watch as the two guys get pushed into the van. Then the brother leans toward the front passenger seat.

"Mom," he says, "can you sit back here, between Sandy's newcomer and me?"

The front passenger door opens, and out steps Mrs. Potato Head. She looks right through my layers of eyeliner and fear.

"Of course I will, honey. Can't have you sitting next to the boys, now, can we Cyndy?"

Oh my God, she's the anti-Azores. She's *so* not the mom who lets you smoke inside. Or outside. Or anywhere. My cigarette fantasy goes AWOL.

The UFO light over the backseat is on. Everyone but me is deep into writing in notebooks. God only knows what they could have to say after being locked in a room for the world's longest Wednesday. But they're all *into* it.

I look out the window as we approach, then slip under, green highway signs. When we pass a blue one that says, "Thank you for visiting Virginia!" and right after it a white one that says, "Welcome to Maryland," I'm suddenly talking.

"Where're we going?"

Sandy's moon face rises from her legal pad.

"To my house, your new host home. In Delaware."

Sandy's mom turns to study me, and my heart does a stutter step. She doesn't say anything out loud, but in her eyes I can read those words: "…a three-day evaluation." For the first time in my life, I close my mouth and look down.

After a while, Sandy's pen makes that quick noise, **shrr-rrip**, saying *The End!* to her writing. She slaps her pad to the floor and turns to face me. This girl would *never* make it in the smoking pit. She belongs in, like, math club.

"Okay, first things first! Now that my M.I.'s out of the way, Cyndy, you can meet my parents. You already said hi to my dad—" he lifts his fingers off the steering wheel and twinkles them at me—"and next to you is my mom."

"Hi, Cyndy," says her mom, with a buttermilk smile.

"That guy—" Sandy jerks a thumb at her brother—"is my brother, but you can't talk to him, because no girls talking to boys before Fourth Phase. You can talk to my parents, though. Call them 'Dad G.' and 'Mom G.' So. Tell me about your first day as a Straightling."

We're out in the sticks where there's no streetlights, but the dome light's still on, showing me my reflection in the window. "As a *what*?" I ask my own face. The right side of my lip is doing the *best* Billy Idol sneer.

"I'm over here, Cyndy. Behind you."

She's waiting for me to turn and look at her. So are her parents. And the guys have all put down their pencils. The whole fucking van is waiting for me. I turn from the window and face her.

"As a Straightling," she repeats. "You know, 'Here at Straight, feel great! Nine to nine, feel fine!'"

She's *singing*. She's singing this "song" that the whole beast sang after eating. And she's hand signaling, too: one arm cuts through the air on "Straight." She flashes nine fingers, twice, for "nine to nine." She actually *hugs* herself for "feel fine."

In three days, I tell myself, I'll be sucking a Marlboro *hard* and inhaling Bridgeport through my nose. But maybe I'll keep this one little piece of the story from the Zarzozas. I don't think this is their kind of song.

When Sandy stops singing, I'm supposed to say something, but I have *no* idea what. Then she talks again.

"Why are you at Straight, Cyndy?"

"Man, I don't *know*—"

"Druggie word!" her brother shouts.

I whip my head around, like, *What*?

And he goes, "Tell her not to look at me! Tell her no druggie words!"

Then Sandy takes over.

"You are not to look at boy phasers, Cyndy. Or other newcomer girls, either, except when they're talking in group. But we'll get to that later. And don't use druggie words from your past!"

"Man, *what* are you *talk*—"

"*Don't* use that word, I said!"

There are two boys right behind me, totally listening to me get *told*. Fuck, if we were in the pit right now, I'd be telling this chick what she could do with her fucking *words*. But here, in a Caravan, twelve hours from anywhere and sitting next to her mom? I do what I did with Jacque, before I grew balls: I press into a corner, shut up, and try to hide. But Sandy's not fooled.

"I asked you why you're at Straight, Cyndy."

It would be too weird to say nothing, when there are six people listening. Plus, it seems like her next step'll be to give me a spanking.

"I—I don't know. My mother brought me."

"Why did your mother bring you?"

"I don't know! I don't *do* drugs! I tried to *tell* them that, but they—"

"Straight is a drug rehab, Cyndy. Kids aren't brought here for having tea parties and going to church. What did you do to make your mother bring you to Straight?"

"I mean, I took off. To—to get away from her husband." Fuck their three-day evaluation. I'm looking out the fucking window.

"Oh, I get it. You were a church-going tea-party runaway. And Saturday nights you read the Bible at an old folks' home, right?"

"No, I didn't say—"

Sandy is laughing, and so is her brother. And the two kids behind me. Even her mom's cough is covering up a laugh.

"If you were brought to Straight, you're a fuckup. Sorry for the language, Mom and Dad, but it's true. You're a runaway, and runaways do disgusting things in disgusting places. So let me ask you again, Cyndy. Why. Are. You. At. Straight?"

Nobody's laughing anymore. They all got quiet at *fuckup*. It'd be easier if they were still laughing, so it wasn't up to me to fill the silence.

"We're waiting."

"I—I really don't *know* what I'm doing here!"

I had no idea I'd started crying. But I suddenly am.

"My mother just *brought* me here. I'm not a druggie, and I only drank *once*. I didn't even *like* it—it made me sick! I was just trying to get away…"

"So you're admitting you overdosed on alcohol," Sandy says.

"Man—I mean, I'm *not*! I'm not *any*thing! You'll see in a couple days! They told me three days. They're gonna see I'm not a druggie, and I'll be *outta* here!"

I'm full-on, snot-river crying now. I don't even care what those backseat boys think. But they're laughing at me. They all are. The parents and everybody.

"I'm not! I'm not a drug addict! Are you listening to me?" I snatch a look at Sandy, to see if she even hears me. "I just had to get away from him! I just *left*!"

It's like we're on separate TV screens. There's me and there's all of them. We're on two different shows, and they don't make sense next to each other. I'm begging them to understand; they're smiling and rosy. I must be going crazy.

"Okay, Cyndy," Sandy goes. "Welcome to Straight."

15

HOST HOME DOORS AND WINDOWS MUST BE LOCKED AND ALARMED

When the van finally pulls into a driveway, the dashboard clock says 11:48. But we can't just get out of the car. Sandy and her brother have to work out their Chinese puzzle of place-switching and door-guarding and pants-grabbing. By the time I'm pulled backward out of the van, the clock reads 11:54.

I'm *carried*, not forced from behind, up the stairs to the G. family's front door. That's what they call it—being "carried by the belt loop." I learned some more new words on the car ride too. The beast is not the beast; it's *group*. And when those kids were standing up and telling everyone their horrible secrets? That wasn't confession or torture; that was *sharing*. Oh, and that arm-shaking, head-bashing shit? When those hundreds of kids' arms were punching the air? That's "motivating." *Motivating!* You "motivate" to prove you want to get called on, to stand up and "share" with the "group." One time Mrs. Skinner, English teacher extraordinaire, told our class about this thing called "spin." It's in newspapers and politics and shit, when they take something bad and describe it in a way that sounds good. Like if the devil said, "Sure is *cold* up there for those Connecticut winters! Why don't ya come check out hell, where it's warm and toasty all the time!" He's not *lying*, exactly, is he?

That's what all these Straight words are. They're spin. But the thing with spin is, the spinner is trying to *sell* you something. If you're in Straight, they don't have to sell you anything, because you're already *there*, with a hand in your pants and big monsters at the doors. So why do they care if you're convinced or not? "Pushed by the ass" or "carried by the belt loop"—it's gonna be done to you. Why bother putting a bow on it?

Anyway, I'm "carried" into the G.'s kitchen. We're inside, and I'm thinking it's time for Sandy to take her hand out of my pants. But instead, she yells in my ear.

"We need to be locked in!"

Dad G. appears. There's a key pinched between his fingers; he slides it into the lock on the door. The bolt **Ka-Klunks** as it turns, loud and clear as a pair of steel handcuffs. Dad G. pockets his key and yells back in our faces, "All locked in!"

Sandy's eyes aren't even wide as she goes to me, "Every door and window is locked with a key. And they're alarmed too. There's no way for you to get out."

It's like, she had to convince herself that I can't get away before she could slide her hand out of my pants. But I wasn't even thinking about escape. I was thinking about fire hazards.

To prove Sandy's point, Dad G. starts pressing buttons on the wall by the door. **Teet!** He turns around and sees me watching him. Then he turns back and cups his hand so I can't see which buttons he's pushing. ***TEE-TEET! TEET! TEET!***

"Alarm on," he goes. At least this time he didn't yell.

After a snack of saltines and water, our next stop is a bathroom. Together. Standing between me and the door, Sandy roots around in a drawer and pulls out a bright yellow toothbrush. It's totally not a handout from the school hygienist; the top part is angled and it's got two racing stripes down the handle. It's a real Reach.

"Here ya go."

She pushes a fat new tube of Crest across the counter toward me, but I don't pick it up because I'm studying the toothbrush. The bristles are tan, and spiked out in twenty directions. It looks like it's been used to scrub floors. Or maybe toilets.

"C'mon, I want to go to bed," Sandy says, jabbing her thumb at the toothpaste.

"Umm, I'm—gonna use my finger."

"Whatever, but that's the newcomer toothbrush. Don't think you're getting another one."

Gross! Would my middle finger work to brush my teeth?

After the Crest is put away, it's time for me to *go*. Man, I've been holding this for fifteen hours.

"I gotta use the toilet," I say.

"Go ahead."

"No. I mean, I gotta *go*."

"Okay, there it is. Toilet bowl, toilet paper."

I look her in the eyes, which feels like getting electrocuted, and crunch my eyebrows down. She gets what I'm saying.

"I stay in the room with you," she says. "At all times."

Okay. I'm in this stranger's house, in her *bathroom* with her. In Delaware, two hundred miles from anyone I know. I'm a prisoner in this house, so I'm *trying* to make myself sound polite. I really am. But I get a tone in my voice.

"Listen. I need to go number two. Can I have some privacy, please?"

But Sandy way out-tones me.

"I am your oldcomer. I'll be in the room with you every minute that we're out of the building. *You* are a *newcomer.* You cannot be trusted. There's the toilet. I'll be watching."

The cold of the toilet seat is a slap on my thighs. I don't want to give Sandy any extra thrills, so after I wipe I just drop the paper in the bowl and hope I got it all.

When we step out of the bathroom, Sandy makes another bullhorn announcement.

"Entering phaser room! Dad!"

We're facing a door that's painted white, but the paint

is thin, like a veil. You can totally see the words they painted over.

SANDY'S ROOM!

It's those bubble-stick letters that only cute girls can do, the kind with the gumballs at the ends. From those letters, you can tell what her room's gonna look like. Canopy bed, ruffled dressing table. There's gonna be a bookcase with more of that writing down the sides, *Sandy's Books*. But it'll be stuffed animals, not books, on the shelves. And leaning on her pile of lacy pillows? A Cabbage Patch Kid. Maybe two. Betcha a million dollars.

As Dad G. comes smiling up the stairs, Sandy digs a thumb in my shoulder. So I move forward. Into her room.

The world stops spinning as the space looms open in front of me.

It's a big room, but—

bare windows

bare walls

bare *mattresses.*

Four of them, right on the floor.

That's it.

No curtains, no posters, no bookshelves. No closet doors, hangers or clothes. Just four bare mattresses and a green plastic Coleman lamp, throwing stripes of light around. The Delaware sky through the big, blank windows is black and blue. The sky is the one thing that makes sense.

As Sandy stands guard at the door, her dad goes around and messes with each window.

"All locked," he says.

He replaces Sandy in the doorway. Then her hand is back in my belt loop, and we begin Act Five of *The Weirdest Shit on Earth*. She gets on her knees, pulling me down with her, and starts crawling around the room. Seriously, she's crawling. One-handed. So I'm crawling too, only I get to use both hands.

Sandy presses her face to the floorboards, runs her hand under each mattress. She skims her palm across a window ledge, then crawls us into the empty, doorless closet. She touches every surface in that nothing room, then pulls her hand from my pants and stands up.

I don't even ask why. She tells me anyway.

"I have to make sure there's nothing a newcomer can hurt herself with. You'd be amazed how much damage you can do with that plastic T that holds the tag on new clothes."

"I'm not gonna hurt myself," I say. "You don't have to do all that for me."

"Oh, I'm not doing it just for you. I sweep the room every night, whether I have a newcomer or not."

"Man, you—you do that whole search thing *every* night? Even when it's just *you* sleeping in here?"

"Of course! I don't know when my druggie self might take

over! Once a druggie, always a druggie. I have to protect myself from myself. And hey, good catch with that druggie word."

I don't know *what* the fuck to say to all that. Luckily Dad G. walks back in, so I don't have to say anything. He drops an armful of stuff onto a mattress.

"Call me when you're ready," he says, and pulls the door shut behind him.

"Okay, newcomer," Sandy says. "Give me your clothes, starting with your shoes. And I mean everything. Including hair elastic. Including panties."

And I do it. What choice do I have? Besides, she's already seen me wipe my butt. You can't get any more naked than that. So piece by piece, I hand her the last shreds of myself. My Keds, my Levi's, my tie-dye. She makes a little pile out of them on the floor. Second to last, I hand over my bra.

"Oh. This, we'll have to do something about," she says, rubbing her thumb on the underwire.

"Whadaya—"

"I thought I told you. Anything damaging will be confiscated. Don't you know how many ways a person can kill herself with an underwire bra? By hanging, with just the straps alone. She could slice her wrists with the underwire. And these sharp hooks in the back? Dangerous as a steak knife. I could keep going. I only have B-cup Velcro bras, so you'll have to go without a bra until your parents bring your humble clothes."

She leans over the pile of stuff her dad brought.

"Here," she says, throwing something blue at me. "Pajamas."

I hold the blue thing up: a boy's button-down shirt, minus the buttons. I put it on backward, like a doctor's appointment dress. I keep my left hand behind me, holding the shirt together like a big flesh button. Then I hook my right finger into my undies, close my eyes, and pull.

My eyes are closed as I hold my finger hook out to Sandy. There's evidence in the crotch of what happened in that beige room. If she sees it, I don't want to know.

A tiny weight lifts from my finger, and this girl has my underwear in her hand. I was wrong. You *could* get more naked. This must be why I'd try to kill myself with a nail clipping.

Sandy's different from me. She doesn't give a *shit*. She pulls off her maroon corduroy shirt and her turquoise-blue, elastic waist pants. She's standing there in the biggest pair of granny panties I have ever, ever seen. The white cotton of her ass is the size and shape of a hockey rink. Maybe she *should* kill herself.

I'm drop-jaw staring as she undoes the Velcro part of her bra.

"Well?" she snaps.

She waves her hand at the pile of clothes her dad dropped, and one of her boobs flops out of the bra. It knocks around a little, looking embarrassed.

"What are you waiting for? Get yourself a blanket."

That's my favorite, when people get mad because you

didn't do what they didn't *tell* you to do. I grab a dark green blanket and cocoon myself in scratchiness. I look out the window at the silver hope of the moon.

"Don't get any ideas," she says. "The windows are locked with a key my dad has. *Dad!*"

I turn back to find Sandy in a long flannel nightgown, the same one I had when I was six. She's picking up the mound of our clothes when the door opens again.

"Here you go, Dad," she says, pinching the hot pink corner of my underwear and sifting them out of the pile. She drops them on top of the bundle, then hands it over.

"Goodnight, girls," Dad G. says, and the room goes dark as he takes the camp light out with him. After the solid click of the door closing, there's a muffled **beeeep**, then Dad G.'s voice again. "Alarmed in!" it says.

In the light of the moon I see Sandy drop down to the floor. She pushes a mattress up hard against the door and says, "Get some sleep. Wake-up's in four hours."

I lie down and pray to disappear.

16

NO LEANING OR SLOUCHING

God must not have heard me, 'cause I didn't disappear. Instead, this morning I'm back in the beast. I mean, *group*. But it's not really me anymore, because I'm not in my Levi's. And I don't have on makeup, and my boobs are all dangly and sloppy under this weird yellow shirt Sandy pulled out of the "phaser closet" in the hallway. I don't know who's sitting here, whose thighs are wrapped in old-lady plaid on this plastic seat. But it is *not* Cyndy Etler.

While we were getting dressed, Sandy pulled a Goody barrette from her bathroom drawer and held it out to me. I already had my hair in a ponytail, so at first I was like, what's the point?

"Nah, I'm okay," I said. "My hair's long enough to stay in the ponytail."

"It's not *for* your ponytail. It's for your bangs."

That's when I almost puked. I looked from the barrette in her hand to the red bumps on her forehead, which were on full display, thanks to a silver Goody. A burning wave kicked my stomach to my throat. She was going to make me look like her and that super-loser, Barrette Chick.

"I—I," I choked out, then swallowed the burn. "I'm not gonna wear that." I sounded feeble, even to myself.

"Yes, you are, Cyndy. Now take it and slap your bangs back, so we have time to eat."

I didn't even argue. That's another reason I'm not me anymore: I am *so* not the yes-ma'am kid. But I took the barrette, thumbed it open, and scooped some of my bangs to the side with it.

"'Kay," I said, taking a half-step toward the door.

"Not '*kay*," Sandy said, taking a whole step toward me.

She unclipped the barrette, tweezed all of my bangs back with her fingers, and scraped the barrette across my scalp, hard. When I touched my finger to the spots that hurt, it came away with blood. You could hurt yourself bad with a Goody, if you wanted to. What the fuck happened to "safety first"?

So that was this morning, before we headed back to prison, a.k.a. "the building." When we get here, somebody's already sitting in the front corner seat. But just like yesterday, I get dragged right up to it, like nowhere else will do. Two seats down, there's an empty chair, but no, I have to be centered in the crosshairs between the barstools and the beast, like the target in a spy movie.

After Sandy moves the girl out of my seat, she sits in this row of empty chairs across from me. There are only twelve chairs over there, which are lined up next to the barstools. God knows why they're set up across from the rest of the "group." Maybe those kids watch the group when staff looks away.

Or maybe they're the super-psychos. As soon as Sandy's knees bend—like, before her butt even hits the seat—she's got both her arms up, doing that "motivating" thing. She's angled toward the barstools, whipping her fists around in pentagrams, like a spastic kid *ooh! ooh!*-ing his hand in the teacher's face. But the barstools are *empty*. She's whipping her fists at *nobody*.

More kids are funneling in. They're like creepy, silent crows descending on a branch. And as soon as they sit, they face the empty stools and start motivating. Every single kid, except one. Me.

From my James Dean lounge—legs out, arms crossed—I see movement at the floor, where my eyes are. It's Sandy's right hand. She's spinning it like a pinwheel by her feet, trying to get my attention. And what a sucker I am: it works. I slide my mouth sideways in a smirk, but Sandy doesn't speak that language. She latches her boiled-egg eyeballs onto mine and then, with flat open palms, she jerks her hands upward, three times, quick. It's what my mother would do in church, to tell her choir to stand. Sandy wants me to stand up? No, 'cause now her jerking hand has gone back to doing spaz arms. She's staring at me, and she's motivating.

I've just finished rolling my eyes, settling back to my

power lounge, when I'm punched in the spine. Know how a fisherman jams his knife in a fish, then slices it right open? It's like that: out of the blue, something sharp jabs my neck and pain rips down my spine. Before I can scream, there are clamps on my wrists and a demon at my ear.

"Back straight! Hands up!" it growls.

My arms are yanked up. My hands flop around at weird angles for a sec, until my brain catches up and I make fists. Now *everyone* is motivating at the empty barstools because I'm doing it too. I'm being motivated.

I deal with it the best I can, by crossing my ankles like, "Whatev." These people just don't get it. I'm not *staying* at Straight. I don't friggin' *need* to do this.

So that's what I look like—half my body on vacation, the other half epileptic—when a familiar voice snaps from behind.

"Song!"

I hear the slap of bodies moving faster. The bottoms of Sandy's chair legs clatter and jump on the tiles. Sandy's going *nuts*, and everyone else is too. It's like a flock of geese blasting into flight at the sound of a gunshot. But here, the shot is a word. "Song!"

And then there's another shot, a name this time, and the geese fall dead around me. Everyone's arms drop; mine are pulled down by the hands clenching my wrists.

"John B.!"

A giant pops up on the boys' side. He's a man, almost. You can see the smudge of beard on his face. Then my demon, whose hands are still gripping my wrists, tells me, "Stop staring at the boys' side."

I focus on Sandy's feet, so I'm hearing, not seeing, when a cannon booms out, "You Are My Sunshine."

And the "group" starts singing it. No joke, every one of 'em. Picture three hundred dead-eyed teens, smiling away and singing this shit. Can you even?

Yeah, there was singing yesterday. But it was like "Country Roads" and "Lean on Me"—lame songs you hear on AM radio. And then they sang those songs where "Straight" was every third word. But even *those* weren't as weird as *this*. We sang this song in *nursery* school.

The next thing I know my demon is moving my hands in shapes that go with the lyrics. I'm trying to twist her grip off of me when I see him.

The guy walking down the group-aisle, next to the mean blond staff girl from last night.

He's—he's Scott Deutermeyer!

He looks the same as he used to when he'd come by my house to see Kim, just minus his perfect, faded jean jacket. My jaw unhinges as Scott and the meanie pop onto the barstools. Then I go kind of whirlwind. All the fucked up shit from the past twenty-four hours—being left in this pit with strangers, spine-fisted into rooms, watched on the toilet, forced to crawl around a floor—it takes over my brain. Without even thinking, I raise my hand while everyone else is singing.

And Scott Deutermeyer—someone I *know*! In *here*!—looks right at me. He smiles like a priest and says, "Yes?"

The group stops singing as I smile huge and say loud, "I know you!"

"Stand up!" my demon bellows.

Hands all around me start shoving air upward with flat, angry palms. But I'm not scared. With Scott's John Stamos–look-alike face here in front of me, I couldn't feel safer. I stand up and say it again. This time, I point.

"I know you! Scott Deutermeyer! You're friends with my sister Kim!"

His smile falls, but I'm too hell-bent to wonder what that means. Scott's gonna save me. He's a staff member, and he *knows* me! He'll take me to that little beige room, and I'll tell him how no one's listening when I say I'm not a druggie. He'll tell the other staff, and then I'll be out of here. Fuck three days! In three *hours,* I'll be free. There's so much happy sizzling out of my pores, I'm shocked the chick next to me hasn't caught on fire.

That excitement fizzles, though, when Scott actually speaks.

"What's your name?" he asks.

As if he doesn't know me. As if our being in this hell hole together isn't a miracle from God.

"Cyndy!" I say. "Cyndy Etler!"

For a second he looks at me, like he didn't quite catch what I said. A few more beams of happy short out.

"Kim Etler's sister?" I try. "From Stamford?"

Finally, his gorgeous face nods. I can hear the sigh in his head, like he's remembering a good dream. *Oh, Kiiiiim.* I don't know what's supposed to happen next, but I wish it was something other than this:

"Cyndy Etler, then," he says. "Okay, Cyndy." Then he looks away from me.

The "LOVE YA, *CYN*DY!" is like a tidal wave. It knocks me back into my seat, and I'm surrounded by an ocean of arms. The demon picks up my wrists, hoisting them over my head, and this time I don't even fight her.

"No going outside on First, Second, or Third Phase!"

"Love ya, Jackie!"

"No talking about what goes on in the building!"

"Love ya, Steve!"

"Hold newcomers tight by the belt loop!"

"Love ya, Sandy!"

We're doing this thing called "rules rap," and I'm motivating. On my own. I look like a total spaz, but I'm so psyched to get called on right now, I'd do *any*thing. Because Scott came back to the barstools after lunch, *without* the blond. This is my chance to get him to actually listen. And then my wish comes true. Scott looks right at me, gives me that smile, and says my name.

"Cyndy E.!"

I sit there with my heart doing fireworks.

The demon behind me—a new one; the first one took a break—knuckles me in the back.

"*Get up!*" she snaps.

Angry arms flap at the ceiling, and their force pushes me up too. I'm the only person standing, surrounded by an ocean of faces.

I should've had a plan for what to say. "Umm…"

"When did you get here, Cyndy?" Scott asks.

"Um…yesterday?"

My guts are being pushed through a sausage grinder. Standing above all those kids and *say*ing something?! When I first talked to Scott, I was hypnotized. But this time, I'm wide awake. God *damn*, there're a lot of kids in here.

"You got here *yes*terday," Scott says. "Maybe a little soon for you to know the rules, huh?"

I shrug. It's the slowest, hardest shrug of all time.

"Next time, Cyndy, I want you to have a rule for me. Okay?"

"Okay," I say to the floor tiles.

"Here's one: 'All phasers must motivate in group.' Remember that."

"Okay."

I'm knocked back into my seat by the crush of "Love ya, *Cyn*dy!" And when my butt hits the chair, it's like my brain switches back on. If Scott's gonna help me out of here, why do I have to know the rules? And why'd he say *remember* it?

The demon snatches my hands up again, which cuts off my thoughts. So I'm sitting here, being motivated, when Scott looks over and gives me a nod. *Just* me, like we have a secret. And with a burst, I get it. He told me that rule as a front, so it *looks* like I'm going along with the program. That way the staff will agree when he says, "She's not a fuckup. She's just a nice, bruised kid." What a great idea!

Knowing I'll be gone soon makes me feel bad for the rest of the kids. They're all stuck in this place for—what, like six months, at least? I can motivate today, since I'll be out of here later. Playing along for just one day? That's the least I can do.

So I put some muscle into waving my arms on my own. Down and then up; down and then up. The demon's hands break off my wrists; she pats me twice on the back. And it feels *good*, like somebody likes me. I keep motivating on my own and almost, *almost*, I feel free.

I'm sitting here with a Styrofoam tray bridged across my knees. The tray has the same stuff on it as yesterday: a piece of bologna, two pieces of bread, and hot veggie fart, plus half a cup of water. And a spork.

I learn it's called a spork when this other staff guy comes out for "dinner rap." He's got black hair like Scott Deutermeyer, but he's taller and meaner. He likes being in charge, you can tell. His name's Matt King. He prowls back and forth, talking a blue streak, I guess because the group can't motivate with trays on their laps.

"How's that dinner, y'all? Mm-mm good? I had *my* dinner at Bonanza, y'all know it? Steak place where you get a tray and can pick out whatever you want? They got a salad bar, corn on the cob, mashed potatoes, tater tots, even. Chocolate cream pie, lemon meringue…and I got one o' them big, brown, plastic cups for my Coke. Raise your hand if you know them cups."

From the corner of my eye I see the chick next to me raise her hand, so I turn a little more, and there are hundreds of hands up. We're supposed to answer that question?

Because I'm stupid, I look back at Matt, and his eyes burn right through me. Pure mean.

He keeps going. "Can y'all hear the hard crack when the ice hits the plastic? The swish of the Coke? Who's thirsty? That's it? Nobody else is *thirsty*? Well, shoot! We been treating y'all too good! Maybe I better hold back your water, huh? I said, who's *thirsty*?"

I raise my hand this time, because obviously, I have to.

"Thought so," he says. "Hey, how's y'all's veggie medley? Those sporks treatin' you right?"

Since my hunger beat my ego, I'm eating the veggie fart. So I'm all hunched over when he says that, trying to scoop the glop to my mouth without spilling. It's hard work. Maybe that's why I hear him say *dorks*. "Those dorks treatin' you right?" Totally stupid, but that's what I hear. I look up, my spoon halfway to my mouth, to see what's up with the dorks. And of course, he's right in front of me.

"Here! A spork!" he shouts. He pulls my wrist into the air. The fart stuff flings off the spoon and onto my forehead. My wrist burns under his hand. His grip is a lot like Jacque's.

"What's your name, newcomer?" he barks.

It takes me a second to remember my own name, swear to God. My heart's beating so fast, it's disconnected from my brain.

"Hey," he says, shaking my arm to make sure I know he's there. "I'm talking to you. What's your name?"

"Cyndy," I get out.

For some reason, that makes him really happy.

"*Cyndy!*" he booms, like a TV preacher. Like, *Jesus*! "*Cyndy*, how's your spork treating you?"

The spork must be the spoon thing with three tiny teeth clenched in my fist.

"Fine?" I ask my feet, so my eyes don't get scorched again by his.

"Fine!" he chirps back, cheerful as Santa Claus. "Cyndy's spork is fine, group!"

I hear some laughs behind me, but they're not a happy sound.

"What a relief! Cyndy's. Spork. Is. Fine!"

What did I do? He's mad now, for some reason. And nobody's laughing. Nobody's making a *sound*.

"Cyndy. Tell me, tell *us*, what *is* a spork?"

It's so quiet I hear chewing noises, the gummy snap of teeth on Wonder Bread.

"Um—is it like a fork?"

He's in my face zipfast, right there, his dark eyes hitting me like punches. He's still for a second, bruising me with his eyes, then he opens his mouth and yells.

"Hey, group! Cyndy says a spork is a fork! Well thanks, Cyndy. C for effort."

He pulls his face away from mine and stands. I'm itching to wipe the food off my forehead, but I'm too scared to move. "A *spork*," he says, as he strides over to the boys' side, "is a cross between a *fork* and a *spoon*. But what's the difference? Who's got a spork for me?"

Hundreds of arms lift their sporks into the air, like lighters during a metal band's slow song. Matt studies his captive audience and walks right past me to take some girl's spork. Then he spins and attacks.

"The *difference*" he roars, "is that your *sporks* have *pussy* points at the tip!" He's jabbing my nose with the pussy points. "Do you see these little pussy points, *Cyndy*?"

Somehow I nod.

"And how come Straightlings can only use sporks? Larry B.!" Matt calls out, before kids can even motivate.

A boy stands up. "Straightlings can't be trusted. We would hurt ourselves with forks."

Matt doesn't ask the group why they'd want to hurt themselves. He doesn't need to.

17

NO LYING DOWN WHILE WRITING M.I.S

Scott never came to pull me out of group last night, to talk to me about what I'm doing at Straight. I haven't seen him since that little nod in rules rap. When Sandy belt-looped me out of my front-and-center chair and wedged me heel to toe in that line of girls, I wanted quick death.

I know how that sounds—poor Cyndy—but I don't mean it that way. It's just the truth. I couldn't do another night in that house, with strangers I wasn't allowed to look at, with the locked doors, the dirty comforters and the rescue mission mattresses. After carefully holding hope all day, I couldn't go back to that cell. I needed to die, instead.

But prayers aren't answered quick like that, so I lived. Sandy pushed me into line, then out to the van, then into her padlocked house. She gave me the dingy toothbrush, watched while I pooped, and crawled me around the floor.

There was one thing different about last night, though. In the epic van ride from Virginia to Delaware, when the dome light came on and everyone started scribbling in their notebooks, Sandy tore some paper from her legal pad and handed it to me.

"Mom, can I have a pencil?" she asked.

"For what?"

"For my newcomer to write her M.I., Mom."

"Oh, of course! Just checking. We can't be too safe."

"You're right, Mom. Thanks."

So then I had a pencil, and Sandy told me what to do with it.

"You're going to start writing your M.I.s tonight."

"My *what*?"

"Your M.I.s. Your Moral Inventories. You'll write an M.I. every night you're on your phases."

"What *is* that?"

"I just told you. It's a *Moral Inventory*. You take an inventory of yourself every night, so you keep on track with your program. This is how we work the steps. Got it?"

I still had no idea what she was talking about, but I don't think Sandy noticed, 'cause she went on like I had said, "Oh, totally."

"It's not hard. You name an issue you're struggling with, apply a step to it, and tell how you're going to fix it. Then you write three goals and three validations. Here, I'll set up your paper for you."

This is what she wrote.

Cyndy E.
M.I. for Thursday 11/21/85

Problem:

How I Will Apply My Steps to This Problem:

Solution:

5 Goals:

1.

2.

3.

4.

5.

3 Good Points:

1.

2.

3.

Then she handed the papers back to me and started writing her own, I guess. So I did what I could.

Cyndy E.
M.I. for Thursday 11/21/85

Problem:
I don't belong here.

How I Will Apply My Steps to This Problem:
What?

Solution:
I'm gonna leave in two days.

5 Goals:
1. Leave
2. See Joanna
3. See Steve
4.
5.

3 Good Points:
1. Good Points?
2.
3.

This wasn't what Sandy wanted. I got a lecture on how I have to take my M.I.s seriously, and if I don't know how to work my steps, I need to ask for help, and most important, I have to write about something that's *wrong* with me. I stared at the back of her dad's seat, feeling extra trapped in this big metal coffin on wheels.

But here's the crazy part. When she read Joanna's and Steve's names, she dropped my paper like she'd been electrocuted.

"Druggie friends!" she gasped. Really. That's what she did. She *gasped*. "Cyndy, are those the names of your druggie friends?"

"What? You mean Steve and Jo—"

"STOP!"

Everyone in the whole van sucked in their breath, hard.

"No! Names! Of! Druggie! Friends!" Her eyes were big as hubcaps.

"Um...okay," I said, *really* not sure where to look or what to do.

So today I need to come up with a problem about myself, so tonight I can write a good M.I. But it's hard to think of anything bad because today's Friday, which means tomorrow is Saturday—day three! If I can get through tonight then tomorrow, sometime tomorrow, I'll be out of this place. No hand in my pants, no fist punching my spine, no claws on my wrists.

Halfway through family rap, which is when you have to talk about what an asshole you were to your parents, a side door clunks open. That's not the shocking part. Staff comes in and out of those doors all the time. And right before dinner rap, a gush of kids you haven't seen all day comes through them, too, from God only knows where. But this time the girl who's standing up, talking about beating the snot out of her brother, sits right down when the door opens. She stares at the back of the group, so everyone else looks too. We all turn to see another act in *The Weirdest Shit on Earth.*

Shuffling across the linoleum is this…creature. This big, dirty human who looks like it should be in a cage. *Two* people, a boy and a girl, are gripping this kid's waistband. They jerk the kid to a stop between the boys' side and the girls'. The kid's so dirty, you can't tell which side he or she is gonna get pushed to.

"Incoming!" the staff girl yells from her barstool.

The chick holding onto the newcomer goes, "This is Amanda T. She's from New York City. She dropped out of school."

You could hear an atom split in that room. Nobody's ever seen anything like this person, this—*girl?*

She has a fistful of bangs sprouting over her forehead, but otherwise, she's stone bald. Her body's a bulldozer: big, square, and filthy. And her clothes are just as mind-blowing. Her dirty jeans are *way* too big—where does she *find* jeans that big?—and they're rolled up to her ankles in big, flat cuffs. On top, she's wearing a black T-shirt under a massive leather jacket. And most amazing of all are her shoes. They're Ronald McDonald boots, but instead of red, they're black. They have big bulb toes, laces that wrap around her ankles, and treads like a wedge of old tire.

The staff girl slices through the stunned silence. "Does anyone know Amanda?"

I look around me. Everyone is staring at her with dead eyes. Trapped in this building all day and night, this is like, the first un-tapioca person they've seen in *months*. But they're all just staring. God. I will *never* become so dead-eyed, I swear. I just have to make it 'til tomorrow. Saturday.

Nobody is saying anything. I guess nobody knows Amanda.

"Put 'er on front row!" the staff girl yells.

"Love ya, Amanda!" the group trombones.

The freak train starts moving, and Amanda's pushed along my row. I hear the tumble-flesh of motivating, but I'm not doing it. I'm too caught up in staring at this girl, at her round, pink cheeks. They stop her in front of my seat.

The girl looks right at me and speaks. "What're *you* lookin' at?"

I jump, coming up out of my seat a little, but nobody notices. They're too busy *Shhh!*ing this Amanda girl. Then I'm gripped by my waistband and hoisted out of my seat, and Amanda's plopped into it. She's the new bull's-eye. I'm **thunked** down next to her, into the icky warmth of the girl they just belt-looped up and out. It's a game of musical chairs, minus the music. Everybody gets a fun new seat. And now, me and Amanda are glued together by interlocking chairs.

Did I already say that the chairs are all linked together? Here, put out your right hand, like it's a cup. Now curl your left hand the same, and flip it over. Lock the fingers on each hand together, and try to pull your arms apart. If you did it right, you can't. That's how they keep the group a *group.* The chairs have metal brackets on the sides that lock them, one to the next. So you're always latched: by the ass to some oldcomer, or by the side to some newcomer.

A boy stands up and starts "sharing" about what a scumbag he is. I'm facing him, but I'm secretly sneaking looks at Amanda. Her eyes undo everything else about her. They're huge and soft and baby-powder blue, with lashes as long as your arm. Cheeks like bubble gum, eyes like innocence—up close, this girl is anything but tough. She could be one of Dawn's baby dolls. What happened to her in New York, on her days not in school? What made her take off her dolly dress and put on grungy armor? Wait, I take it back. I don't want to know.

18

EVERYONE MUST WEAR SHOES AND SOCKS

Something weird is going on. Something even weirder than the regular daily freak show. I can feel it. I can hear it. I just can't *see* it yet.

Other than Amanda showing up, it's been a normal day—people singing stupid songs; kids sharing about their druggie pasts; the teen staff strutting to the barstools like they're on the red carpet. But then the side doors open, and all these kids I've never seen before come flooding in. They stand around the edges of group, wedged tight at the shoulder in a human fortress. It's creepy and just...wrong.

A half hour later, on some invisible cue, they swarm around us, claw us up from our seats, and carry us across the group room. The door goons are gone, so they march us right through the back doors and into this empty room. The walls are bare brick and the carpet is new-jeans blue. We're tugged into rows, because with no talking allowed and no chairs, how do we know where we're supposed to sit? We should know, though. I can tell by the way my carrier is yanking me around. She practically tears my belt loop off.

Once we're all positioned and sitting cross-legged—with the boys' side so close, if I whistled, I'd ruffle their bangs—the bad guys show up: Matt King and the mean blond smiler.

"Family rap!" Matt yells.

The people around me start motivating and I do it too, because I don't want a fucking demon at my back. Without anyone telling me, I put my arms up and shake them around. And that's what gets Matt's attention. He's scanning the tightly packed room, and his eyes sear into me. They look even darker than yesterday.

"Cyyyyndy," he goes.

The blond staff snaps her head my way. Her smile blinks to life.

"Oh! Y-yeah?" I say back.

My fists are still up by my ears. This isn't what I was motivating for. I didn't actually want to be called on.

"Stand up!" he says, fake friendly.

Everyone's palms do the upward air shove.

My rubbery legs make it hard to stand. It's silent except for the rustle of my clothes.

"So…?" Matt says from his barstool.

"What?" I say back. But I say it confused, not snotty.

"*What?* What. *What* is that this is *fam*ily rap. You need to tell us about an incident from your past, an incident involving your family."

Four hundred eyes and chins are leveled at me. They make it hard to think.

"Um…"

"Were you a good girl in your past, Cyndy? Were you nice and sweet to your family?"

"Well, they—"

"I'm not asking about *them*. Were *you* nice and sweet to your family?"

"Um, no?"

"That's right, Cyndy! You're doing great. Now tell us about an incident with your family where you acted like your druggie self."

I just stand there. I don't have a family. I have a mother and a sister and a stepthing who's the devil, plus his kids. And "an incident"? I have no idea what I'm supposed to say.

"CYNDY ETLER!"

My whole name. He says my whole name. Like he has some…*owner*ship of me.

"Yeah?"

"We're waiting!"

"I—I don't know."

I might be starting to cry a little.

He's still staring at me, his eyebrows pointed into sharp little horns.

"I thought I'd give you another chance, Cyndy. But you've wasted enough of this group's time. Have a seat."

I can't sit down fast enough, so I fall instead. My hand catches a girl's shoulder, but she jerks it off like she *hates* me. I feel it, like a heat.

The group starts to yell a "Love ya—" at me, but Matt cuts them off. "No!"

Next the girl who hates me stands up, to share how she made her father beat her. "I remember, this one time?" she starts out.

That's Straight code for, *Here's why my parents hate me enough to leave me here.*

"I remember saying to my dad, 'Maybe if you didn't drink so much, Mom wouldn't need therapy.' I said that to my *dad*. I ended up in the hospital with a broken arm after that sweet nothing. And I deserved it, one hundred percent. He fed me and clothed me and kept a roof over my head, and that's the thanks I give him? I can't believe he'll even still look at me."

Matt doesn't just let the group tell her *Love ya*, he *leads* it. Before she even sits, he's all, "Love ya, Sammie!" so loud it rattles the doorknobs.

At the end of family rap, Lucy tells us what song she wants to hear—one of those ones from Sunday school. It goes, "They will know we are Straightlings by our love, by our love. They will knoooow we are Straightlings by our love."

The next slap of weird comes when they push us back into the never-ending beige of the group room. The linked chairs are still in rows, but they've been turned around to face an *ocean* of gray folding chairs. There's enough seats for all of Communist China. It's like a chair warehouse, which, *ding*! That's what this place is! It's a warehouse, literally. It's a giant storage locker where, for a fee, parents can disappear their fuckups and rejects.

That's another reason I'll be outta here tomorrow. No way does my mother have the money for this place, when she can barely put five dollars of gas in her car. Twenty-four hours, and I'll be on my way back to Jo's; forty-eight and I'm in Steve's room. How could their parents *not* let me stay with them, when they hear what I've been through?

I can *feel* my Levi's on my thighs, my denim on my back. Just *thinking* about Levi's feels so good, I barely notice that I'm picking up a dinner tray and getting pushed back to the chairs. In my mind I'm like, one hundred percent in Levi's…until the hand in my pants lets go while I'm still standing.

"Uh?" I kind of grunt, turning my head to the demon behind me.

"Go down the row," she says. "Sit in that first open seat."

Feeling like the balloon some little kid let go of, I look down the row, and oh my God! It's not the front row! I'm out of the bull's-eye!

"Thanks," I say.

I get a mean *Shhh!* for a reply, but it's drowned out by this earsplitting **screech**. Since I'm standing, I can see what's going on. But, God. I wish I couldn't.

It's Amanda. She's surrounded by demons, and she's fighting them all at once. Crouched at her back is the biggest guy you've ever seen. He loops his arms around her from behind, linking his hands in a hate hug. But even worse is what they're doing to her arms. Two guys are gripping her wrists, Jacque style. Matt King style. They're spreading them like airplane wings, out and down and fast. Tomorrow she'll have handcuff bruises. She's telling them she hates them with animal sounds, not words. I don't know if I'm more scared for her or for them.

A fist hits my spine, so I move down the row. I'm trying not to hear it all: the screams, the *thwap* of flesh on flesh, the shriek of metal as a kicked chair scrapes across the floor. When I get down to my seat, I can't help it. I look back at Amanda right as the big guy snaps his hand over her mouth. He's—he's gagging her. Her face is red, and it's getting redder. Her eyes bulge out, and she *slams* her head forward, then back.

There's a **crack** as her skull hits his, and a **SHREE!** as Amanda throws opens her throat. She head-cracked the gagger. She got his hand off her mouth.

"Gimme my fucking Doc!" she screams.

She rips her bare foot away from the guy who was pinning it; he lunges and tackles her shin. Other guys are running at her. That's when I sit down. I sit and pray for somewhere to put my tray, so I can plug my ears. Amanda's noises are shredding me. It's like she knows what she's doing, fighting off all these guys. This is why she needs armor clothes. I don't want to see or hear or know that it's happening again.

"Intake room! Sit on 'er!"

It's our hero, Matt King. He's striding across the room. He's calm, he's casual. He's *happy*.

There's more fleshy struggle sounds, more running feet.

"Group. Look," Matt says, in a voice you don't ignore. "This could be you, if you try to run."

We spin around to watch Amanda, who's being carried across the room by six guys. She's a human casket. She's got one boot on, and her body's rippling, trying to shake the boys off her. And she's howling.

"Gimme my Doc Marten, you cock-fucking bastards! I'll kill you! I'll—"

Another guy runs over and jams a hand over her mouth. His teeth glint through his smile.

In English class, one of Mrs. Skinner's vocab words was "maxim," which is a wise little phrase about life. She gave us this example they use in Japan, to make sure everybody acts the same as everybody else: "The nail that sticks up gets hammered down." Amanda is the sticking-up nail. But she's not smooth and straight, like a regular nail. She's all knotted up. They can't hammer her flat, so they're killing her instead.

The funeral procession ends as the boys carry Amanda through a door to the left of the kitchen. It's a beige door, painted to match the walls, like they don't want anyone to know it's there. The door slams; the group room's silent. It sounds like the end of the world.

19

OPEN MEETING INTRODUCTION: NAME, AGE, DRUGS, HOW LONG ON DRUGS, HOW LONG HERE

Twenty minutes after the Amanda horror, people are eating their bologna and bread like nothing happened. But a ton of people are eating with their left hands and making Cs with their right. And for the first time since I've been here, nobody is talking. Nobody's singing. It's a silence you could choke on.

So these C-hands, hovering over people's laps? They're even creepier than the other crazy shit in here. Because why is everyone staring straight ahead? Why are they pretending not to notice the creepy C-hands? Not everybody is doing a C, but most are. Like, should I be? What does C mean?

There's a side stander moving from C to C like a bumblebee looping from flower to flower. The side standers are human blockades, like the door guards. Only they stand right next to the chairs at the edge of the group, instead of in front of the double doors. I guess they're there to beat you up, if you try to run.

The chick next to me has her hand up in a C, so a side stander comes over and squishes herself between us. I don't know why she's almost on my lap, but it feels nice. Safe. Like she likes me. But she's not here to talk to me. She's leaning in, so the girl with the C-hand can whisper in her ear. The side stander's pen scratches on her pad, which is tilted, so nobody else can see the words. Then she flips the page, stands, and is gone, bouncing on to the next C, leaving a cooling stripe along my thigh.

Another side stander is going down the rows too, but this one is stopping behind every chair. Like a piston, she plunges her fist down the back of each kid.

"Back straight! Feet flat!"

Plunge.

"Back straight! Feet flat!"

Have you ever been in your backyard right before a storm, when nature clicks off, dark and silent? You're kind of freaked—where'd the birds and sun go?—but you want to stay out because it smells so good, and the breeze is on your face, and it's better than TV. Who cares if you get wet? But then the thunder pounds in like an army, and *crack!* The lightning's right there, like it came for you. You race into your house and slam the door, then realize you're trying to lock out lightning. So you laugh at yourself. You laugh, but your heart is still pounding, and your gut is still frozen. Because really. If lightning wants you, it's gonna get you.

I've got that same helpless dread, trapped here in group, with the back-plunger approaching and the C-hands hovering. But here, there's no door I can lock. And whatever is after me, it's way worse than lightning.

And just like the storm, there's a **crack!** like the world splitting open. Snapping my head up, I see two guys, splitting the room in half. They're dragging this massive accordion door across the room, turning it into a wall, separating us from the warehouse of folding chairs. The guys are straining like pioneer oxen under this 20-foot-tall door. If that thing fell off its tracks, it would crush every one of us.

As the boys get the door to the far wall and latch it, the rest of the storm kicks up. Trash barrels get rumbled over; dinner trays get passed down the rows. The sudden action after breath-held silence is terrifying.

Then the side door pushes open and staff comes filing in. But it's new staff, *dressed* staff. I'm talking men in suits and ties, and women with those floppy silk bows around their necks. These staff are grown-ups; I've never seen them before—except for the one black lady. Mrs. Harper! *That* fucking lady! She's shoulder to shoulder with these other sharp dressers, looking like she sleeps just fine at night. They all look that way. Like they've never taken a wicked crap in their life.

I will never be one of those people. I don't care how old

I get. I will never look like—no, I'll never look *at* kids this way. When I'm a grown-up, I'll still be wearing Levi's and cranking *Sticky Fingers*. I'll blare it from my Jeep, revving dirt on these poindexters and jamming my middle finger in the air.

There are five of them, this fancy new staff. They're staring out over our heads like they're deep in prayer. But not me. I'm studying them good. Other than the evil Mrs. Harper, the only one that's interesting is this tall, tan guy. He could be twins with Erik Estrada, he's so chisel-faced. His black hair stands up straight on his head, and he's got cowboy boots on. *Orange* ones. What's his deal?

When grown-up staff comes striding in, the group gets infected by their pompousness. Even without fists in their backs, people stiffen and sit up. They turn their chins forward and put their hands on their knees, perfect and squared-off as a row of dominoes.

When fancy staff are done staring at the wall behind us, Orange Boots lifts a clipboard and speaks. He sounds like a robot. "Terri A.: talk."

And the group hammers back at him:

Clap-clap-clap!

The claps are military-tight, like they're made by a machine.

"Gina A.: talk."

Clap-clap-clap!

"John B.: talk and responsibilities."

Clap-clap-clap!

It keeps going, just like that. The grown-ups give some code, and the group understands and replies *clap-clap-clap!*

Then Orange Boots says, "Tara D.: going home."

The girl next to me gasps. Seriously, she's sitting in group, and she makes a *noise*. I whip my head left as she clamps her hand over her mouth. The rest of her face is a mess: hot red, with her eyes all squinched into knots.

The group goes *clap-clap-clap* and the demon behind us whispers, "Eyes forward!"

Tara D. and me jerk back into position.

"Mike F.: third phase."

Clap-clap-clap!

Tara *D*. and Mike *F*. They skipped right over E, for Etler. But that's fine. I didn't want to talk to anyone, anyway.

The listing and clapping goes on and on, and then, as Orange Boots and crew turn to march out, my old friend Scott appears. He's in a jacket and tie, and Jesus, he shined his friggin' shoes.

"How 'bout a song?" he says.

Over the motivating, I hear other sounds: creaking and scraping and voices coming from behind the accordion wall. Scott calls on some girl who says, "The Rose," and the noise is drowned out by the group, moaning about how love is a razor.

There are other words to the song, but I can't understand them. Nobody can. The group is doing a megaphone version of that pudding-mouth mumble you do when you're only pretending you know the lyrics.

We sing an easy one next, "Zip-a-Dee-Doo-Dah." Some dude suggests it, and Scott goes, "Okay. Five times," before zooming off to the side of the room.

Two door brutes start yanking back the accordion wall as the group is snapping its fingers, miming smiles and sunshine, Zip-a-dee-doo-dah-ing for the—

the—

the *avalanche* of grown-ups looking at us from the other side of the room. Listen to me. There's a *million* of them. And they're—they're all singing "Zip-a-dee-doo-dah" too.

In the days I've been here, I've never been this freaked. I've known that I'm alone in a mob of psychos, but I've never felt *this* alone. I'm a tiny speck in this universe. Half the people around me are out to get me, and *all* of them are acting like this shit is normal. Grown-ups doing sparkly motions with their fingers? I've never been so friendless, so *unprotected* in my life. I can't even feel God right now.

So I do the best I can to make myself invisible. I follow—perfectly—the rules I know. I make my spine a metal rod. I bolt my feet to the floor. In between Zip-a-dees, I cup my hands on my knees. I'm perfect. In my foam-green corduroys and burgundy button-down, I'm one of them. I hope.

I can't squeeze my eyes shut and pray to a God I don't feel, so I try something else. I pray, I guess, to the group: please, don't notice me. Just do your weird thing, and pretend I'm not here.

My prayer and "Zip-a-dee-doo-dah" end at the same

time. The ginormous room is silent. Nobody moves. Not the kids on my side, not the mass of grown-ups across from us. We just sit and stare at each other, like, *Who's gonna blink first?*

Then Scott appears, holding a microphone. He walks the long stretch of floor to the center of the room with the mic in his hand, stopping once to lasso-yank the cord free.

"Welcome, parents and guests, to open meeting, November 22, 1985. Tonight Tanya R. will be sharing her story."

Then he loops back and hands the mic to the girl in the bull's-eye seat. She takes it as she stands.

"My—" **SCREET!**

The whole grown-up side of the room dips their heads and shoots their hands to their ears. But the group side? We don't even flinch. We're frozen, hands on knees, like we didn't even feel our ears split. Like we're not even human. Tanya pulls the mic from her mouth and tries again.

"My name is Tanya, I'm fifteen, and I *do* believe I'm a druggie."

I guess I'm allowed to look at her, since she's talking. I risk a glance around, and yeah, everybody else is, even the guys' side. So I turn toward her voice, and I'm staring at the homecoming queen. Even without makeup, even with her bangs slapped back, this girl is gorgeous. She looks like Skipper, Barbie's little sister. She looks like the kind of kid who still *plays* with Barbies while her dad reads the Bible and her mom bakes brownies. Fuck her.

"The drugs I've done are pot, alcohol, hashish, hash oil,

Thai stick, Thai weed, cocaine, LSD, uppers, downers, and trash drugs…and heroin."

Say *what?* This is a joke, right? This is *Candid Camera*. Without even thinking about getting in trouble, I totally look at everybody else. But nobody's laughing. The group is frozen, and the grown-ups are nodding with pressed lips, like, "I told you so." But, oh my God, she's lying! This girl has never smelled a cigarette! Man, what the fuck? I mean, Amanda? Amanda's done some shit. Amanda's copped a trash drug in her day, whatever *that* is. But this chick? No way.

Tanya's still talking. She's mastered the mic; the lies are just *rolling* through her lips now.

"I've done these drugs for two years, and I've been straight for two weeks. The incident I'd like to share tonight is from the night of my junior prom. I was supposed to be elected prom queen."

I *told* you! She *was* prom queen!

"Everyone had said they were going to vote for me, but my druggie friend won, instead. I felt hurt, and confused, and angry. I felt that my whole druggie school lied to me, which made me feel…lonely, I guess, and I…"

Scott appears on the sidelines again. Real loud, he says, "Wrap it up, Tanya," while circling a finger over his head.

Tanya's face becomes a beet, and she gets all speedy.

"So after the prom, I went to a hotel with my druggie friends and ended up meeting these older men who gave me alcohol and downers. I took so many pills that I should be dead right now. I took twenty-six pills, and then I went swimming in the hotel pool—"

Scott's circling pointer goes up again. It's the only movement in the room. Now Tanya *really* cranks up the speed.

"—and I had sex with all of the men, and I'd be dead now if my parents hadn't put me in Straight."

She plunks back into her chair in a haze of shame and bullshit. And I have this total psychic moment where I'm reading this girl's thoughts, her scrambled egg thoughts, through the back of her skull: she can't believe she said all that to six hundred people. Seriously, I *know* this. She's like, I did *do those things, didn't I? I'm a druggie, and druggies do gross stuff and black out. So I must've done those things that night. I must have.*

God's back with me, I guess, giving me this psychic-ness. To apologize for abandoning me. Why I'd want this gift, I couldn't say. But I'm sitting and hearing Tanya's brain in my head, and I'm dying to ask her why she lied, when a lady and a man stand up across the divide. The lady's holding another mic.

"Damon?" she asks in a teetering voice, and a kid springs up from the guys' side like he's on fast-forward. "Damon, I—"

The lady starts bawling, in front of all these people. The man pulls the mic from her hand and starts barking.

"Damon, I swear on God's name, you won't set foot in my home until you finish this program. I am goddamn *sick*ened by you. You had us fooled, didn't you? Honor roll, baseball scholarship… You really pulled the wool over our eyes. When executive staff told us what you were up to, your mother cried for *three days*. Good thing I didn't know where your host home was, because I wanted to kill you. I went into your room, instead, and cracked all those druggie records you're so proud of. They're in bits all over your room for you to clean up, if you ever come home. If you don't work this program, son, you'll no longer *be* my son."

As Damon's parents sit down, the grown-up side of the room starts clapping. The kind of clapping that makes your palms hurt. And poor Damon yells, "I love you, Mom. Love you, Dad," but he's crying. He's standing there, in front of six hundred people, crying.

Then another set of parents vaults up from their chairs and, on fire from the roasting of Damon, start yelling the same kind of stuff at their kid; the kid calls back that he loves them. Then it's a girl's turn. Then another guy. The parents are all reading the same script: we hate you, we hate you, we hate you. And the kid just says back, "I love you."

But every once in a while the script changes. Like when Prom Queen Skipper's parents stand up.

They go, "Tanya, we're so proud of you." And then—you ready for this? Her dad starts crying. Her *dad*. "We're so grateful we have our little girl back," he calls out. "Thank you, Straight, Inc.!"

That makes all the parents clap and stomp and whistle and

cheer. And the group does too. The clapping party goes on for like five minutes, until Scott yells, "Okay, parents. Let's move on…unless you want to be dismissed at 2:00 a.m.?" Everybody laughs at that, and the grown-up side mic starts moving again.

Some of the parents just go, like, "Love you Tom," and pass the mic real quick, like a hot potato. The cord on that thing must be a million miles long.

Then there's big excitement when this one mom stands up. "Tara?" She says it as a question, like she's not sure Tara is in the room.

And the chick sitting next to me springs out of her seat and screams, "*COMING HOME!*" Then she friggin' *jets* across the divide between the group and the grown-ups.

You can't even imagine it, this blaze of a girl plowing through the throng of parents. She gets to her mother and the two of them stand there, clutching each other and sobbing. It's kind of touching. I mean, that's obviously a good mom, so Tara's lucky she gets to go home to her. And God, is she lucky to be getting out of here!

All the grown-ups must think so, too, 'cause they're stupid grinning at the two of them.

Then killjoy Scott, my used-to-be crush, steps into the middle of the room and says, "Wrap it up, Tara." So in other words, quit having the best moment of your life, Tara.

Tara peels herself off her mother, then gallops back to her seat. But wait, I'm confused. I thought she was going home.

I'm staring at Tara, trying to read *her* mind, when the lightning bolt strikes.

"Cinny?"

He's *here*.

I fold in half at the hips. I don't know where I think I'm going, but I'm *not* letting Jacque see my face. Instantly, hands are pulling my shoulders back and forcing my body up. In this mob of staring strangers, I'm standing here, chained in place by demons, exposed to my mother and Jacque.

He's talking into the microphone. He's saying, "Love you, Cinny."

The clutch of hands pressing me from behind won't let me drop and hide.

Then my mother speaks into the mic.

"Cyndy, I—I've been so scared for you, so scared *of* you. And now you've become a—" She stops to put her head down and cry. Strangers' hands rise up around her, patting her back and arms. They feel bad for her. Her plan is working. She lifts her face and keeps going. "And now you're a *druggie*. I hope you'll do the program, Cyndy. I love you."

Something inside me scorches, hot and high, before it drops into a cinder. It must be my heart. I fall back so hard, so fast, I punch right through the hands.

"Stand up!" Scott yells—a verbal spanking.

I stand. In front of me, the blue chair is fascinating.

Scott says, "Mom, Dad, will you stand back up? Cyndy, tell your parents you love them."

The only sound is skin fighting skin as I try to fall back again. But these chicks behind me aren't letting me sit down. No way.

My mind reels back to Amanda, thrashing around the floor like an unhooked carp as the brute boys pinned her down. Amanda didn't win. I won't, either.

So I say it. What the fuck else can I do?

"Love you," I say.

Ol' Scott, he doesn't even need the mic, this time. We all hear him perfectly.

"Louder!"

Drowning in the spotlight, I swallow my hate and yell my first lie.

"Love you!"

The hands finally let me collapse into my seat, but the fist at my back makes me sit up. Proper, iron-spined. Straight.

20

NO ANIMALS IN THE BUILDING

In the deep parts of the ocean, I bet there's no such thing as time. It's just dark. You swim past rocks and plants in one long, continuous night.

That's what the days in Straight are like too. You can't tell time is moving when you're trapped in a windowless warehouse all day. The only clock I see is the minivan's, which says 8:50 when we get to the building in the morning, and 9:30 or 10:00 when we leave it at night. So the average day is twelve, thirteen hours in group. But this day for *real* feels like infinity.

We must have sat in that mega-group with all the parents for four hours. Now I'm in a mini-group with, like, fifty girls, while the other kids are off doing their "talks." At least that's what Scott yelled out, as they were pulling the wall closed again.

"Talks, come on. Fifth-phasers, grab a talker."

Certain kids were carried by the belt loop to the parent side of the closing wall; then the leftover oldcomers started unlinking chairs, pushing them into the opposite corners. Girls on the left, boys on the right. But these chairs aren't being put back into rows. They're in a messy semicircle, so each corner looks like a Shakespearean theater. Us girls in the chairs are facing a barstool where Lucy, the mean blond smiler, sits. That's her name, Lucy. As in, "I Love."

We sit in the same creepy silence as before the parents came, when everybody had their C-hands up. We're watching Lucy sit with her legs crossed, cutely dangling a shoe and silently reading her little papers. She has a whole stack of them, and they must be good, 'cause some of them make her raise her eyebrows, and a few times she's gasped, "Oh my gawd." One time she lifts her head and stares *right* at the girl behind me. I don't know what that was all about, but I'm *so* glad it wasn't me she was staring at.

Sitting here, I have nothing to do but rip apart that scene with my mother. Why the fuck was she trying to sound like these other kids' parents? "Do the program"? She must not *know* they're cutting me loose tomorrow. Druggie, my ass! She's been scared of *me*?! How 'bout *me* being scared of *Jacque*?! Yeah, okay, "Mom." Once I'm the fuck free, I'll hitch back to Bridgeport and disappear. She'll never have to be scared of me again.

I must have smoke coming out my ears, 'cause Lucy's watching me. I look up and there she is, staring. And smiling.

All the talkers are being brought back to our side of the room, bawling and snorting up their snots. This girls' corner of chairs is filling up. Shit, some of these talker chicks are motivating even before they're sat down, while they're still hooked to their oldcomer leash. So I start motivating too, because I'm *not* getting in any more trouble tonight.

And then they're all back, and they're *pissed*. I can feel their hard energy crackling through my arms; I'm picking it up like antennae. They're—*we're* motivating at Lucy, who's cleaning under her nail with a folded slip of paper. She's ignoring us, so the fury is ramping up higher. Girls are using serious muscle, snapping their arms for attention. And it's contagious. The harder one girl motivates, the harder everyone else tries to out-motivate her.

On the boys' side, they're beating us all. The clank of metal on metal comes from their corner. I twist to look through the flesh forest, and it's like a demolition derby over there. The boys are tearing it *up*, motivating so hard their chairs are bashing into one another. *Jesus*, their fists are cracking each other's heads, and they don't even seem to—

"*Cyndy Etler!*"

My heart slams down to my seat.

At the sound of my name, the arm forest drops, just like that. The girls' side of the room is staring at me as I touch my right hand to my heart like, "Who? Me?"

The scariest part of *The Wall* is when Pink Floyd has a whole symphony playing backup. The instruments start deep and dark, then switch to a screaming high. You know the part I'm talking about, right after the piano's playing tears and the voice begs to know what he did wrong, to go home… Then comes the key in the lock. The door creaks in; the bad guy is *right there.* And then the steps start. It's a bassoon pounding left-right, left-right. The judger is coming, heavy. The shriek of the violin goes up, up, tearing you open from your z-z to your throat.

And the judging starts.

Lucy's using her good-times voice.

"C'mon, Cyndy! Stand up! We want to get to *know* you!"

The violin is telling me to run, run somehow, run somewhere. Just, disa*ppear.* But I can't. I'm hemmed into place by a sea of blue chairs, by the girls packed into them. By the side standers, circling the blue. Girls and girls and girls, their flaming eyes fixed on me, me with my bruised-up spine. Locked in position in my chair, my left fist still up by my ear. But I'm—I'm motivating! I'm doing what they want!

"Stand up!"

The words rip out of Lucy, jerking me up from my seat. I'm in the spotlight again as hands fill the air, grasping and clawing after me. My head feels like it weighs a hundred pounds, way too heavy for my neck, so I face the floor, like maybe the answer is written on the cold hard tile. What did I *do?*

There is one thing I know: these people hate me. The force of that fact hits me like a falling piano. I stumble under its weight, and my weakness feeds the beast. A clawing hand rips at my arm; a fist pops my head. Girls' bodies convulse in their chairs; they're spitting through clenched teeth. It's a feeding frenzy. The beast is starving. I'm the meat.

Lucy whip-cracks a name—"Karen S.!"—and I don't move. I can't get in trouble if I don't do anything, right?

Some girl springs up out of her seat. M-maybe she's gonna be laughing. Maybe this is a joke they play on the new kid. Maybe this Karen S. is gonna say, "Ha! We gotcha! Just kidding." So I look up.

I've never seen this Karen girl before, but her hand is in the shape of a gun. A gun pointed at my face.

"Cyndy Etler! You need to get honest with this group! Why do you think you're here?" Karen's getting madder as she goes. My eyes are burning from looking at her hate, so instead, I look down at her feet. Which are scrambling to get closer to me. She's so close she could choke me. She keeps going.

"You're a druggie, just like me! You—"

"Siddown, Karen," Lucy says. She's disgusted, like Karen did something wrong too. What'd *she* do? What'd *I* do?

Karen sits, *fwump*. I snatch a look at her and see a shaking, dull-eyed girl. My God, she's as scared as I am.

"Someone else!" Lucy yells.

Someone needs to do a better job of killing my soul. Lucy has spoken; the fists and claws are spinning again. Karen is motivating the hardest of them all. She wants her second chance.

I'm standing still in the middle of this hell storm. I'm standing extra, extra still.

In that judging section of *The Wall*, when everyone tells the prisoner how much they hate him, something important happens: he realizes he's crazy. And all the angels sing the word, right alongside his crackly, beaten voice, like that was God's message all along. You're crazy, and it's all been your own fault.

You'd think everyone would love the prisoner then. For being such a good boy, for realizing it's *him*. But they don't. The prisoner confesses; the crowd gets crueler. The guitar rips through the judge's rumbling, sneering voice. The way he spits his words, you can tell the judge *loves* this: brutalizing innocents. He's tickled pink.

And the judge does the cruelest thing possible: he throws Crazy to his peers. He tells the bloodthirsty pack of them to tear Crazy down. There's hundreds of them. Millions. Cheering, ripping, trumpets laughing. They're drunk on the thrill of tearing the sad Crazy to shreds.

Lucy swivels back and forth on her barstool, pushing off the footrest with her toes. She's like, the cutest girl at the birthday party, with a pinafore on and a balloon in her hand. Lucy's the friggin' devil.

"Who's next?" she calls.

The girls go even harder. A drop of someone's sweat pings me on the nose.

But Lucy ignores them. She's playing with her slips again, smoothing the edges and pulling them tight, blind to the riot scene in front of her. She stays that way, I swear, for five whole minutes. Ignoring them. Ignoring me as I hang there, a body on a noose. Finally Lucy looks at me, a blond eyebrow pushed up by the thought that just came to her.

"Sandy?" Lucy says her name like it's a question, the same way you'd answer the phone.

Up lunges my oldcomer, Sandy. Her Cream of Wheat skin is pulled tight, and it's purple with rage. She's crackling and snarling, a brand-new Sandy.

"*You!*" The word burns up from her throat, and the boys' side is suddenly quiet. "You think you're so special!"

My stare is off the floor now. I'm looking right at her, because I'm scared what will happen if I don't. Her fingers, curled around the chair-back in front of her, are shaking so hard the chair's rattling. *With* the fat girl sitting in it. Jesus.

"You think you're so young and cute, Mommy's going to swoop in and save you!" she yells.

"Cute? M-mommy? No, that's not—"

"SHUT! UP! Shut *up* with your druggie fantasies! Your own *moth*er is *scared* of you! We all heard her say it! She knows you're a druggie! *We* know you're a druggie! *You're* the only one with your head still up your ass!"

Some laughter sails over from the boys' side. To my right, a girl starts motivating. Her breath goes **CHUKKA-CHUKKA**.

Lucy cuts them off with a high-pitched, "*'Ey!*" The **CHUKKA**er puts her hands down; the boys' side shuts up. Lucy smiles at Sandy. "Go on," she says.

If you can believe it, Sandy gets louder. "My *parents,*" she yells, "have *welcomed* you into their *home*!"

She's pushing past the knees and rows of girls between us. My God, she's coming to get me.

"And you—you *disrespect* them!"

She's one chair-back away from me. She's right here. With the same instinct that taught me to hide from Jacque, I take two stumble-steps back. And I'm arm-cuffed by a demon. It's the same one who squeezed up next to me, earlier, to take notes on her pad.

That's what Lucy's been reading up there. The notes from when people were making Cs with their hands.

The demon locks my arms behind me, then forces me back toward Sandy. Sandy, whose hand will be gripping the back of my pants later tonight. Sandy, who's yelling in my face as the whole girls' and boys' sides watch.

"You shit on your parents in your druggie past, little girl. But not now, not my parents! Druggie words in their car?! Druggie friends' names?! Saying you'll be *leav*ing after three days?! Ha! Dream on!"

She cleared her throat with that *ha,* which hurled some gunk up onto my cheek. My arms are strapped to my sides, so Sandy's throat-snot stays where it is.

Then Lucy pops the balloon.

"Okaaaaaay, Sandy! Thank you!"

The boys start motivating across the room, and Sandy's face pulls away from me.

In the movie of *The Wall*, you know the prisoner's cooked at the end of his trial. He's no longer a person. He's a floppy rag doll, stitched empty circles for eyes. He leans broken on the wall, no life in him to fight off whatever's coming next.

I'd lie broken on the floor if not for the demon note-taker holding me up. I wonder if she smells Sandy's snot on my face. I wonder if she smells what happened in my pants. I wonder, but I don't care. I have nothing left to care with.

"Love ya, Sandy!" the group screams.

Everything's back to normal. The boys are still motivating in their corner; the girls start motivating in ours. Everyone's pretending this face-rape never happened. Everyone but me and Lucy.

"Are you going to be good, Cyndy?" Lucy asks. "Can my fifth-phaser let go of you?"

My eyes are dried out blisters underneath my clipped-back bangs. I drag my head up to look at her, and Lucy smiles.

"Oh, yes," she says. "You'll be good. Go ahead and drop her, Samantha. But stand at the end of her row."

"Looooooove ya, *Cyn*dy!" the group tells me.

When the trial ends in *The Wall*, your speakers explode with the thunder of bricks blasting open. Then it's almost silent. The chanting and cheering are over; all you hear is the sharp trickle of brick bits raining to the ground. And there's a kiddie instrument, a recorder or a kazoo. It plays the saddest, slowest song.

Hands rise as I sit down and bring my chest to my knees.

Fists whip through the air. Girls plunge up and down in their chairs. The *tsch-tsch* of heaving breath surrounds me in stereo, and the demon Samantha is back behind me, reminding me what to do. She clamps my wrists and lifts them, and I'm motivating. I'm asking Lucy to call on me again. Please, Lucy, let it be me.

Lucy studies her C notes. She flips the top one to the back, and scans the next page. She gets a huge grin on her face and looks at that first girl who screamed at me.

"*Karen S.!*" Lucy shouts.

The girls' side goes nuts.

21

NO RADIO, TV, OR READING ON FIRST OR SECOND PHASE, EXCEPT FOR BIBLE ON SECOND PHASE

Today is Saturday. It's day three of my evaluation, which I obviously failed. It's the day my mother was supposed to be coming for me, because I'm *so* not a druggie, no matter what these freaks think.

Last night, after that crushed-in-the-corner torture rap, Sandy came over and grabbed me by the belt loop, like nothing had happened between us. She brought me to the pyramid of jackets, and that's when I saw the bags. Thirty paper grocery bags with folded-over tops, all lined up on the floor, with names written on them in Magic Marker. One had been kicked to the side. It had my name on it. It knocked the wind outta me.

It was my mother's handwriting. No doubt. Plus, nobody else spells my name right, with two Ys. So...when my mother came for that giant meeting, she brought me a brown paper bag. If she was going to pull me out of here today, why did I need a paper bag?

That bag means—it means I'm not—I'm not getting taken out of here. I'm gonna be here for this whole never-ending day. And the next one, and the next and the next. Because it's totally my mother's choice, if I'm in here or not. You can't escape when there are hands in your pants and alarms on the windows and goons at the doors.

My mother knows I don't belong here. She knows I ran away because of her husband. But she won't say that. She'll say I'm a bad girl, a violent druggie, because this setup is perfect for her. She gets to be Poor Nadine, whose daughter is a terror. Poor Nadine, whose kid made her life a living hell.

She's not signing me out of Straight, Inc. She's leaving me here. Instead of bringing me home, she's giving me this bag.

I looked at the green digital clock when I climbed in the minivan last night, after the parent meeting and the torture show in the corner. It was 1:49 a.m. We were in group for *seventeen hours.*

Here at Straight, feel great! Nine to one forty-nine, feel fine!

I asked Sandy's permission to open my bag, but of course she had to open it for me. To "search the contents," to make sure my mother hadn't sent me a joint or a bra with knife hooks or something. Instead of drugs, Sandy pulled out these clothes that were unreal. Seriously, they looked like they were made for a cartoon character. There's nowhere on earth you can buy shit that looks like this, but somewhere, somehow, my mother made it happen.

Here's what she gave me:

- A *size sixteen* pair of pants made from cloth that looks like denim, but isn't. They have an elastic waistband and no pockets. She's getting me back for just *ev*erything, with these pants.
- Another pair of pants, but made of friggin' velour, the color of cinnamon. Also with an elastic waist. Also size sixteen. I mean, does she think I'm pregnant?
- And another pair that are like, make-you-cry ugly: turquoise-blue polyester, with a stitched line going down the front of each leg. *Bell*-bottoms. Size…you know.
- Three slippery button-downs with triangles and lines all over them. They're brown and yellow and marmalade, like I want to look like Connecticut in November. Guys named Chico get these shirts for a quarter somewhere.
- Twelve pairs of plain white tube socks, and

> these—I don't even think you can call them sneakers. They're shoe-shaped Tupperware. They're white, they're plastic, and they close with a big Velcro strap. *Velcro.*

"Your humble clothes are an important part of becoming a Straightling," Sandy told me. "You need to humble yourself by wearing clothes that are the opposite of your druggie image. Before long, you'll come to hate your old druggie image. You'll see."

You can't *not* hate yourself if you're wearing Velcro sneakers.

"Oh! One more thing," Sandy said, looking into the bag and sounding truly happy. "How nice Mom Etler is! She sent you an allowable treat."

My mother used to put surprises in my Easter basket and stuff, when I was little. That "allowable treat" was the first nice thing my mother's given me in like ten years. I wanted so bad to slap Sandy for being the one to find it.

She pulled out a roll of Life Savers.

There are, like, three things I know about my father. One, they chose *his music* for the opening concert at fucking Lincoln Center. *Very* big deal. Two, he brought my mother yellow roses all the time. And three, he loved Butter Rum Life Savers and hated the mint ones, like I do. The roll in Sandy's hand was white with glistening green letters. Wint O Green.

That's when it hit me like a hard left hook to the brain: my father. That's how my mother's going to pay for this place. She's using the money my father left me for college and the social security checks I get because he's dead.

I wrote my Moral Inventory last night about hating mint Life Savers.

"Your M.I.s will get better as you learn your program," Sandy said. "But you need to start thinking about your real issues, and use your M.I.s to work on those. Okay?"

I made a throat noise and kept my nose on the window. But Sandy didn't push it. Guess she's only a badass in group.

"So, did you get what happened today?" she said, handing our dangerous pencils back to her mom in the front seat. "This was a typical Friday. Fridays are always late nights, because we have open meeting *and* review. Mondays we have review too, but the parents and siblings have their own raps separate from us. I'm sure you've figured out that raps are intensive discussion groups, where we face our deepest issues and hold each other accountable, right?"

She went yipping on and on, one of those little dogs that barks the whole day and you're like, *where do you get the energy*? Here's what I learned:

1. Those people standing around the sides of group? The side standers? They're called fifth-phasers. They've been at Straight the longest—we're talking a year, at *least*—and

they've "earned trust." Sandy's words, man. The fifth-phasers hardly have to be in the building, 'cause they go to school or work, plus they get four days off from group a week. But when they're in group, they're the demons, the cops. That's why they punch you in the spine to make you sit up and why they were motivating me. They're also the only ones allowed to talk during raps, which is how they could take the "concerns."

2. Concerns. That's some scary, tattletale shit. When everybody had their hands cupped in that creepy C shape? They were trying to "report a concern." That's what you do when you think somebody's breaking a rule and you want to narc on them. The concerns get brought to staff on little papers. The concerns are turned into bullets and shot back at you in Review.
3. Review is the spin-word for last night's firing line, when I was stood up in the back corner and spit on for, according to Sandy, "abusing her parents with druggie words."

Now you might want to sit down, before I tell you this next thing. When people were screaming at me last night, a millimeter from my face? When Sandy hocked a loogie on me? That was on purpose. That's—are you sitting yet?

4. Spit therapy. Sandy didn't explain spit therapy. I guess it's obvious how *that's* supposed to work.

I really, really listened when Sandy explained all of this. I need to understand how shit works in this joint. No moment with Jacque was scarier than standing there, trapped by an army of hate soldiers. It was...it was...listen, I'll do whatever they want, *anything*, to not have to stand up in review again. I've just got to figure out what these Straightlings want from me, so I can make myself invisible.

When Sandy finished her orientation lecture, I could tell I was supposed to say something. But what? *Hey, thanks for spitting on me in review?* Jesus. It was right then that this car pulled up next to us at a red light. The driver turned on his dome light to look for his smokes or something, and there, dangling from the rearview mirror, was an air freshener that—*God*, it was just what I needed. A little piece of me, back.

"Look! That air freshener! It's a Stones tongue!"

"*Hey!*" Her voice snapped my rush in half. "Druggie symbol! You *know* not to—"

"But it's an air freshener!" I said, jamming my finger against the window and drinking in its smooth red curves. Home, that's what that Stones tongue looked like. *Home.*

My chest started heaving and I totally started crying. It came on so fast, I couldn't stop it.

"Don't look! Get down! Get down on the floor!" Sandy was furious, but she was scared too. I could hear it in her voice. So I squeezed down onto the minivan floor. The hubbub behind us told me her brother was pushing his newcomers down too. Like, what the *fuck*?

I inched my face up from the floor mat and said, "But it's not, like, the Stones' *music*, it's just—"

"Stop it! No druggie groups!" Her hair was flying loose from her barrette, she was so freaked.

Okay. Got it. No druggie symbols, no druggie music, no air fresheners. In that one car ride, I learned all *kinds* of important stuff.

So now it's my third day. I'm back in group, and so is Amanda. She's back on "front row." That's what Matt King called it when he saw Amanda this morning: "Put her first seat, front row." Front row. Close cousin of the famous "death row."

Amanda came into group today looking like an old man at death's door. Everything about her was slow and slumped, and there was only one female oldcomer's hand in her pants. It's like they drained out all of her fight. I would think they'd drugged her, if we weren't in a drug rehab.

But here's what's awesome: even if she can't see it, Amanda is the one who's winning. She's still got on her Levi's, 'cause where are they gonna find some polyester humble pants that fit her? And they can't slap back her quail tuft with a barrette, 'cause there's nothing to clip it to. The rest of her head's bald. So here's Amanda, all druggied out with her punk-rock hairdo and her ripped-up jeans. First seat, front row. A three-hundred-pound middle finger.

The second Amanda is put in her chair, some side stander—I mean, some fifth-phaser—starts motivating. We're not in a rap; I don't even think it's nine yet. Oldcomers are still carrying newcomers through the side door, and no one's on the barstools. But this fifth-phaser's motivating hard. Like, snapping fingers and jumping feet. Damn.

You *know* Matt King sees her, but he's talking with the Erik Estrada guy, back behind group. He's not gonna be bothered. Still, the fifth-phaser keeps going, motivating her ass off at the empty stools.

Amanda's settled in her chair now, beef-arms crossed over her druggie flannel shirt. The fifth-phaser is snapping away, while everyone else is just quiet. Maybe they're thinking about how Amanda looks like Rambo visiting a preschool. She's color *way* outside the lines.

Oh, and here comes my best friend, Lucy. Her pointy silver flats **snap-snap-snap** across the tiles. She sure is happy to be Straight staff today.

"Sam Lancer! Sam, do you have something to share?" Lucy calls out as she walks.

Now that I'm allowed to, I turn and look at the motivator, at Sam Lancer. What I see is shocking. She's *brown*, man.

I didn't think any of the kids in here were brown. And she's gorgeous, even in stupid clothes with her hair slapped back. But this chick, she's an *animal.*

"You!" Sam blares out. "You with the druggie hair!"

We all know who she's talking to, and that person better stand her ass up. I try to use last night's psychic trick to communicate with her, like, *Amanda, come on! You know what happened in review last night—*

Except, Amanda *doesn't* know what happened in review last night. She got carried through that door next to the kitchen, and she didn't come back out. So she doesn't know about spit therapy. She doesn't even *know* what druggie hair is. And—she doesn't know what's about to happen to her. Oh my God, Amanda.

"Stand up!" Lucy shouts.

And I duck, no lie. It's like Lucy's yelling at me. It's like it's still review. And I guess it kind of is, only now it's review for Amanda.

Lucy's reached the front of group. She's standing in front of Amanda with her stonewashed ankle-zip Guess jeans. Feet spread, fists on hips. If you put each of them on a scale, one Amanda would equal three Lucys. But Lucy is *way* the fuck scarier than Amanda. Way.

"What's your name?" Lucy barks.

Amanda's not looking up at Lucy, no way. Her powder-blues stay locked on the ground.

"Hey! I'm talking to you!" Lucy says.

She flicks Amanda's ear, hard, like it's a taped-up paper football.

My stomach churns; my butthole clamps back a disaster. Amanda is so fucking dead. She's gonna roar out of that seat and tank Lucy, and then they'll kill her. These people will fucking *kill her.*

But Amanda doesn't roar, or tackle, or even move. God, what did they *do* to her in that room?

"Make this newcomer stand," Lucy snaps, and instantly, two fifth-phasers yank Amanda to her feet. To her black-socked feet. So they got her boots last night. Fuckin' A. They won.

Amanda doesn't fight them. She lets herself be hoisted, and when Sam Lancer starts motivating again, Amanda lifts her head. Her eyes are still blue, but they're not soft anymore. It took Straight one night to kill the softness.

"I already called on you, Sam," Lucy smiles. "Go ahead! Share with us!"

And the beauty starts screaming at the beast. "I don't know where you come from. I don't know what you *are*. But I *do* know how your druggie *hair* makes me *feel."*

This Sam girl is yelling and pacing along the side of group, and she's crying. Her voice is all chokey. She swipes her top lip with her fist, gathering the snot that's pooled there.

"I used to be like you! I used to have druggie hair like that, pretending I was tough! But I—"

She stops a minute to sob, and another fifth-phaser puts

her hand on Sam's back. When Sam looks up, she's not brown anymore. She's dark, blood-red.

"When I had druggie hair like that, I was a fucking *slut*! I let men do whatever they wanted to me, and I *hated* myself! And I am angry, I am so, so *angry* that you brought my druggie hair into this group!"

Sam can't talk anymore. Her fingers are covering her eyes; the bottom parts of her palms are crammed in her mouth. I can see her teeth bite into them. She'll have scars to show.

"Love ya, Sam! Love ya, *Amanda*!" the group screams.

Sam's *love ya* is melted honey. Amanda's *love ya* is snake venom. I never knew the exact same words could say the exact opposite thing.

Everyone's hands are up now, and Matt King is standing at the barstools with Lucy. Lucy looks at him with her eyebrows raised and shrugs, which makes the group go harder. Including me. I go harder too. The fifth-phasers are pushing Amanda back into her seat, but the group is still motivating. They want her. They all—we all—want to *get* her.

Matt sneers and looks right at me. "Nah," he goes. "No time. We'll get 'er later."

It's just before lunch when Matt finds the time. "Fifth-phasers!" he shouts. "Take a look at your group!"

He pauses, letting the paranoia sink in.

"You need to scrutinize every member of this group, and make me a haircut list. Who's building their ego off their hair? Who's going back to their druggie style? I don't care what phase they're on. A fifth-phaser can slip as quick as a first-phaser. We all know it!"

He claps three times, so hard I see sparks.

"I want those lists up the chain of command and in my hand by noon. Got it?"

A half hour later a lady comes in, spreads a bedsheet behind group, and puts one blue chair in the center of it. Then it's time for lunch rap. We all line up by the kitchen and wait there as Matt flips through his little papers. Finally, he calls out a name.

That kid gets walked from the lunch line to the chair. The lady raises her scissors and she snips. And snips. And snips. The kid in the chair gets more and more naked as we watch; the lady keeps cutting 'til Matt tells her to stop.

"Okay thanks, Mom Z.! Annnnd...who's next? Oh, I know: Amanda! Amanda T., come on dowwwwn!"

And we all stand and watch as a single sharp snip takes Amanda's tuft away.

Just like Matt promised, "We'll get 'er later."

22

NO LEAVING GROUP WITHOUT STAFF PERMISSION

After leaving the building at 1:49 a.m. on Friday, we hit Sandy's at 3:55. We were in the phaser room on the mattresses from, like, 4:00 to 7:00. I had three hours of "sleep opportunity," and Straight says that's enough. If your body was horizontal for three hours, you got enough sleep to stay in group for twelve hours. To keep us awake, they do a late-afternoon phaser rap, which is pretty much the blueprint of hell.

John, a barrel-shaped staff with a donut of blond hair, yells out, "First phase!" He's a seal trainer swinging an anchovy.

Arq! Arq! we squeal with spinning hands, reaching for that prize: a chance to stand up and share when you're *not* in trouble. That's the trick. If you motivate without a ton of energy, you're "hiding in group." And if you're hiding in group, you've got something to hide. And if they think you're hiding something, you'll get concerns. So you've got to *always* motivate like a lunatic, like you're *always* on fire to share. But if you can share a Straight rule, rather than talking about yourself, you're totally safe. Or at least, mostly safe.

"First phase rules!" says John.

"All newcomers carried firmly by the belt loop!" a boys' side seal yips out.

"First-phasers speak only to staff, oldcomer, or host-parent!" cries a girl.

"First-phasers live at host home!" says a boy.

"No phone, TV, music, or reading, except for M.I. and program rules!" says a girl.

"Second phase?" John yells.

"In building, all day, every day!" says a very happy boy phaser.

"Live at home, must take newcomers!" says another.

"No lying down while writing M.I.!" says a third.

"Only on *second* phase, Jack?" John says, in a not-so-happy voice. "So you're looking forward to third, fourth, and fifth phases, when you can lie down while you write your M.I.s?"

"No. I didn't mean—" Jack gets out, before John cuts him off.

"Third phase!"

Jack looks confused, like he's not sure if he's allowed to sit or not. But when another guy stands up, he sits down in a flash.

"Out of building *only* to report to school or work!" the guy says.

I guess Jack is okay, because John keeps calling on other people. But how do you *know* when you're in trouble for being wrong? And how do you know when you're safe?

"No talking to non-Straightlings at school or work!"

"May watch G-rated movies! May read program-approved materials!"

"Fourth phase?" John says.

"School or work, plus one evening and one weekend day away from the building, to prepare for being Out There."

Out There? That girl totally pronounced it using capitals. If you ask me, being *in here* is what's Out There.

"Permissions must be okayed: first by parents, then by staff, and requested 72 hours in advance."

"Phasers must be chaperoned on outings by parent or host-parent."

"And fifth phase!" John shouts.

"School or work, and four days out of the building—adapting to Out There."

God! What is Out There—another planet?

"May request unchaperoned permissions for church."

Once we have all that clear, we switch to a new game: whack-a-mole.

"Okay, guys," John yells. "We're gonna mix it up. When I call your name and a number, stand up and shout how long you were on that phase. And no 'love ya's. Let's make this snappy. Okay...second phase! Olivia R.!"

"Four months!"

"Third phase! Jack M.!"

"Six months!"

"Mmm...fifth phase! Billy B.!"

"Which time around? First or second?"

The whole group laughs at that. Bent over, knee-slapping. Everyone but us on front row. We don't get the joke.

"Both times!"

"Fifth phase three months, setback nine months; fifth phase, round two, six months, so far!"

They all laugh again. That kid's been here...holy fuck, *eighteen months*—and that's only since he got on the last phase? And they all think this is *funny*?

"First phase! Sandy G.!"

"Twelve months!"

Her words are echoing in my brain, and still, the group's fucking laughing. My oldcomer was on *first phase,* with a hand gripping her pants, carrying her everywhere she went, for *twelve months*?

"That's almost hall of fame, Sandy!" John tells her with a giant grin. "I thought I had it bad, with eleven months. Who's got Sandy beat?"

Twenty hands fly up, at least. Oh my God, I can't even hear this.

"John V.?"

"Five days plus thirteen months!"

"Max W.?"

"Sixteen months."

Max W. isn't laughing. If you ask me, Max W. kind of looks like he could cry. If he does, I will, too.

"Tanya R.?"

"Ten months!"

"Who *beat* Sandy's twelve, Tanya? Who had a *longer* first phase?"

"Oh. Oops!"

The laughter rolls again. There're a few claps and a "Love ya, Tanya!"

This is what having a good time looks like at Straight.

Matt had last night off, but he's been making up for it with a vengeance today. We're doing "Row Row Row Your Boat," but he struts to the barstools as if they're playing that Stones song—I mean, just, um, that song, "Hot Stuff."

"Generic rap!" he goes, before people can motivate at him. "Talk about *anything*. What's on your mind? Cyndy E.?"

This can't be happening again. Can it?

I force my legs to lift my body, 'cause it'll be way worse if I don't stand right up. I—I'll try. Just please, God, don't let them hurt me.

"How ya doin', Cyndy?"

"Fine?" I whisper back.

"She's fine, group! Who's glad Cyndy's fine?"

Hands rise.

"So glad you're settling in. Whatcha gonna share with us this evening?"

"Um…I…"

"Come on now, Cyndy. You've been here, what, three days now? Surely you've got some thoughts and feelings to relate."

"I…I…"

That's all I can think to say, with all those eyes on me. A minute drags past. I can feel the weight of their stare.

"Tick-tock! Nothing to share with your group? Everyone here is trying to help you face your druggie past and get sober, and all you can do is stand there and stutter? Hell, if I were still in group, I'd have a lot to say about that!"

Hands are back up, starting slow, moving faster. I can see the swinging arms from the corner of my eye: a swarm of them, girls' side *and* boys'. Everybody's out to get me, except Amanda and Max W. Amanda and Max W. *Amanda'n'MaxW. Amanda'n'MaxW.*

"Sam L.?"

Amand'n'MaxW. Amanda'n'MaxW.

"…think you're lily-white?"

Amanda'n'MaxW.

"…a little baby-druggie. Well guess what, little one? Your mommy's not here now. But *we* are."

Amanda'n'MaxW.

"…gonna make your life a living hell!"

"Well said, Sam. Cyndy? Have a seat."

"Love ya, Sam! Love ya, *Cyndy*!"

You wouldn't believe how many things you can say with a "love ya."

"Who's nex—hey! Amanda! *Love* the haircut…stand on up and show us!"

Maybe to keep our minds from snapping, on some Saturday nights, staff gives the group something fun. Only *some* Saturdays, though; Sandy can't stress that enough. And they almost *never* do movies. She didn't get one single movie for her whole twelve months on first phase. And my first Saturday night I not only get a movie, but I get *The Outsiders*?! Sandy was so pissed, she was shaking.

Watching *The Outsiders* was unbelievable. I forgot my iron spine and pinched knees for almost two hours. I was *gone.* I was in Bridgeport. That movie is totally me and my friends. My badass, loyal friends.

While watching *The Outsiders*, I knew. I knew, in that psychic way, that Jo and Steve were coming to bust me outta here. That's what hood friends do, right? When one is fucked, the others will do anything to help, because we know that nobody else will. I just gotta be ready to run, when my outsiders come crashing in.

On Sunday mornings we get to actually sleep, because we don't go in to the building until noon. I was pretty psyched when Sandy woke me up at nine instead of six, so when Mom G. gave us breakfast—eggs and grits—I tried playing their game.

"Will you ask him to pass me the salt?" I said. I was totally facing Sandy, not her brother or the salt shaker in front of him. She loved it.

"Of course! Nice job! Here you go!"

So I'm figuring out how to get through this. It's like doing math equations.

1. Following their rules + Talking about yourself in group = Surviving
2. Surviving + Being ready for Jo and Steve = Getting the fuck outta here

I can do it. I just have to wait for those guys to come get me, while fooling everyone here into thinking I'm one of them. I have to act like a zombie Straightling. Until I'm sprung, the group needs to love me. They'll shout, "Love ya, Cyndy!" without dragging the o out like *yeah, right.*

And thank you, God, it's working! In rules rap today, I motivated and got called on and yelled out Scott's rule. "All phasers must motivate in group!"

The group said back, "Love ya, Cyndy!" like they meant it, and it felt *good*. It felt…safe.

When I sat back down I motivated extra hard, the way people did in review. I didn't get called on again, but that's okay. They can tell I've changed.

And listen, I learned an easy way to talk about yourself in group: you "relate." When someone else is talking about a time they slapped their mother, took money for sex, or blew pot smoke in their parakeet's face, you stand up too and say, "I can relate, because this one time I did x, y, z." You only need one or two sentences because the first kid's already shared his guts out.

Good thing I figured this out, because otherwise, all I'd be able to share would be, "Uh, this one time I tried to smoke pot, but I didn't know how, so I burned my lips really bad. After that I kept a pipe in my pocket, to pretend I was a pot-smoker."

I also wrote my first okay M.I. tonight. Sandy liked it, but she said starting tomorrow, I have to fill up two whole pages.

Cyndy E.
M.I. for 11/24/85

Problem:

I love druggie bands, and I keep thinking about them.

How I Will Apply My Steps to This Problem:
I will apply the first step to this problem. I will admit that I am powerless over druggie music.

Solution:
I will ask a power greater than myself to take druggie music out of my head, and I will listen harder in group.

Five Goals:
1. Earn Talk.
2. Earn Second Phase.
3. Stop thinking about druggie music.
4. Relate in Group tomorrow (4 goals!)

Three Good Points:
1. I gave a rule in Rules Rap!
2. I asked my oldcomer to ask for the salt for me.
3. I admitted I am powerless over druggie music.

Sandy wasn't that impressed by my four goals—all she said was, "Nice goals, but you need to have five tomorrow"—but that's fine. I don't even need her to be proud of me. I'm proud of *myself.*

23

NO BREAKING ANYONE'S ANONYMITY OR TALKING BEHIND ANYONE'S BACK

There's this cool thing we do in group, to talk to other phasers without actually *talking*. Here, you try it: take your right hand, turn it sideways, and press all your fingertips together, so it looks like you're about to do shadow animals on the wall. Got it? Now flare all your fingers apart, hard, so it looks like your hand is exploding. **BOOM!**

That's how we tell somebody in group, *Wake up!* You have to be aware of whoever's sitting around you. If they're in their head, or rocking out, you need to call them on it. It's especially awesome when the zoner is sitting right next to you, because you get to put your fist right in their face. But then, as soon as you fling your fingers open, you have to look right back at whoever's sharing, because no eye games in group.

Correcting someone with hand signals makes it obvious

that you're doing everything right. And if you're doing everything right, they can't stand you up in review.

Another helpful hand signal is this: tap both pointer fingers by the sides of your eyes, then shoot them toward the person sharing. That's for when somebody's looking at anything other than the person talking. But if someone's looking at one of the doors, that means he or she is thinking about copping out. Then you get to put your hand up in a concern and report them to a fifth-phaser.

It's amazing how much you can say without talking. Since I started paying attention, I've learned so much. When someone's not sharing loud enough, you push one palm upward, to tell them to speak up. And if they say, "You can't hear me?" from over on the boys' side, you shake your head no and point at your ear. If someone mentions a person who's not there, you put your hand over your shoulder and pinch your fingers and thumb together like Pac-Man, to show "talking behind backs." When someone's going on too long in group, you spin one finger over your head, like, *Wrap it up!* And of course, if somebody's refusing to stand when they get called on, you put both hands over your head and push upward, like *Get up, ya fucking jerk!*

If the person who won't stand is sitting next to you, you get to actually push them up until a fifth-phaser gets there to take over. I know because this fourth phase girl—wait, I can't talk about a specific person. That would be talking behind backs.

Okay, um…a setback happened yesterday, from fourth phase to front row, and there was a refusal to stand. So I got to do what was done to me last week, when hands on my back and armpits forced me to stand up. When I was pushing to make standing happen, I felt—I'm not sure if this is okay, but I felt *great*. Like I had a little bit of my Hulk back. And Lucy saw—I mean, I was seen forcing standing, so I know that it's known, that I've changed.

And now the whole group knows how different I am, 'cause I related today. For the very first time, I stood up and shared about my past. An incident was being talked about, about learning how to smoke cigarettes. And I put my hands up into the stone-still air and I motivated. Just me. It was major.

"Cyndy E.?"

I stood.

"I can relate to you?" I said, facing the—facing—turning in the direction that sharing had been done from. "I can relate because me and my friends—"

"Your *druggie* friends?" I was asked from the barstools.

"Oh, yeah. My druggie friends. We totally hung out in the smoking pit, and like—"

"Watch the druggie slang, but keep going," was said.

"Huh? Oh. Um, we—we wouldn't be caught dead in the cafeteria. We didn't eat, we just smoked."

It felt like there was something else I was supposed to say, but I didn't know what, so I sat down. "Love ya, Cyndy!"

was said by the group, so I guess I did okay. And I think I can say "group," since it's not a specific person. So, see? I'm learning the rules, and I'm fooling the group. So I'll be okay 'til I'm rescued.

Okay, this is a new one: "girls' rap" and "guys' rap." It can't be review. It better not be! It's only Monday afternoon! But they're separating us—I mean, we're being sep—I mean, separation is being done. Ah, fuck it. I would never talk behind backs out loud, 'cause that'd get me executed. But when the group can't hear me? Fuck it. I'm talking like a normal human.

So us girls are brought back to that carpeted room where they stored us, Friday afternoon, to set up all those chairs for open meeting. We're put in a circle on the floor. We're all sitting cross-legged, but Lucy is perched on her barstool. And I get sat right next to her.

Lucy's hair is a yellow triangle, same as always, but today she's got this silvery-pink lipstick on, plus so much mascara her lashes are tarantula legs. I've never noticed all this makeup, but I've never been this close to her, either. I'm so close I can see the question mark on her Guess jeans' pocket when she stool-spins her back to me. I fucking hate her.

There are no guys guarding the doors, which is super

weird, but to make up for it, the fifth- and fourth-phasers are standing around us. I don't recognize a lot of the fourth-phasers, because they're not in group much. Even when they are, they're sitting in those chairs across from front row, so I don't mix with them.

But this one girl who's standing right over me? You'd think I'd have noticed her, since you can hardly tell she's a girl. Her hair is plain brown, and it's cut like the Little Dutch Boy. She's covered with freckles, as if she's a starry night. And there's something about her, her body or clothes or *some*thing, that makes her seem guyish. So I'm sitting Indian style, motivating *and* looking at this fourth-phaser, trying to figure out why she looks like a boy, when the sleeve of her shirt slips down and I get a good look at her arm.

Okay, listen to me. You have to do this. Lay your arm out so your hand is on your knee, with your palm facing upward. You see that big stretch of skin there? Feel how soft that skin is, like a helpless baby? That part of this chick's arm is covered with thick red slashes that spell F T W. The big line of the F is dug into her elbow crease, and the end-slash of the W crosses her wrist vein. This chick must have been on-another-*planet* high to knife herself that deep and not die. And what *happened* to her, to make her feel "Fuck The World" *that* much? Jesus! I've heard of bowl burns, but this is something *else*. Who the fuck am I in here with? I am *so* out of my league.

I don't want to look at Lucy, and I can't look at this

fourth-phaser anymore, so I'm staring at a nice patch of carpet when I hear Lucy call out a name. A girl stands up. And, *man*! Am I as ugly as these chicks? This one who just stood up has a Frankenstein head. It's square, and her hair's the length of a postage stamp. Her lips are bright pink and their edges look scratchy, like she spends all her time gnawing on them. And this is how bad she looks *before* I check out her humble clothes.

"Girls' rap!" Lucy says. She's hyper again today. "It's just us girls, so lay it on the line! We're talking, *sex*. What'd you get good feelings off of in your druggie past?"

"Well..." Scratchy Lip says.

She's in no hurry to share with us. Is she going to talk about sex? For real?

"C'mon. We all did it. Gotta get off on something. What was it for you? Did you use a banana? Did ya...jerk your brother? Spill it!"

"Well, I don't really..."

There it is. The girl's upper teeth start grinding into her lower lip. Does that feel good, like scratching an itch? Good enough to be worth the dry red crustiness the rest of the time? Like, have you ever heard of ChapStick?

"What do you mean, 'you don't really'? There're no virgins here. What's the matter? Don't you trust your group?"

The girl is still gnawing. "But I mean, I really didn't..."

When I was in the fourth grade, this kid brought his Transformers to school. He let me hold one, and it was the coolest thing ever: its whole *face* twisted around. When the Transformer was human, it had a regular mouth with an almost-smile. Then you spun its head, and it turned into the evilest robot-guy ever. It could gnash you into splinters with its fangs.

Lucy is that Transformer. She does the exact same trick. Her face totally flips from friendly counselor to psycho killer. Oh my God, she's jumping down from her stool. She's so close to this girl, she could gnaw her lip for her. Her knife nail jabs against Scratchy Lip's shirt.

"You better get honest, phaser," Lucy growls. It's a voice you do not fuck with.

"Oh—okay," Scratchy says. She does my trick, the stumble-step. "You're—you're right, I've been full of shit. I need to get honest."

Seagull arms rise and flap meanly, like they're gonna tear into Scratchy for daring to keep her secrets. But Lucy shakes her head no at them. "Good," she tells Scratchy, and goes back to her stool.

The poor girl chews for a sec, like she's thinking.

"I—I did sex with my dog," she says. She's burning the carpet with her stare. "I was—um—I was desperate for drugs, but I didn't have any. I had to get good feelings off something. There was nothing to eat in the house, and no alcohol, so I put peanut butter on myself, and..."

I am totally not lying to you. The chick is fucking *saying* this! And Lucy's face Transformers back into friendly counselor. She's smiling at Scratchy again, nodding. The angry hands are down at people's sides, and everyone—everyone but me—is looking at Scratchy with "Good girl!" in their eyes.

Where. The fuck. Am I? Steve, you guys need to *hurry the fuck up*.

"John B.: talk and responsibilities."

Clap-clap-clap!

"Misty R.: talk."

Clap-clap-clap!

It's a short list tonight, and I'm not on it. I really thought I'd get talk, 'cause I've been doing so good. Sandy knows that, better than anybody. But when she was writing a progress report on me last night, I asked if she thought I'd get talk.

She said, "I don't know, Cyndy."

So I snuck a look under her arm and saw this:

Progress Report For: Cyndy Etler

Asking for: Talk

Deserving: Nothing

I should've known I'd get nothing, rather than being stupid hopeful. Now I'm smack in the middle of review, front row. All the chairs are in a giant C around the barstool. We're waiting for the talkers to get back, and some fifth-phaser's relating about her day at school. But really, everyone's thinking about the concerns in Lucy's hand. Everyone except me.

I'm thinking about how my mother's only a wall away. Every Monday and Friday for the first three months, parents and siblings have to come for family raps. It's one of the rules. So if I had earned talk, I'd be sitting with my mother right now. And I *know* if she looked in my eyes, she'd change her mind about leaving me here. She'd see how crumpled I've become in five days, and she'd feel horrible. She'd take me away. She'd take me home. Wouldn't she?

I don't care how bad that house was. I didn't know bad until I met this place. I've learned so much since I got here, like what drugs do to you and what a troublemaker I was becoming. I'll be a totally different kid when she brings me home. I'll never fight with Jacque, and I'll do good in school. I'll tell Jo and Steve no thanks when the bowl comes around, and I'll drink Yoo-hoo when they drink Bud.

My mother is right here in the building. She's got to feel the vibe I'm sending her. She just wanted to scare me, and it totally worked. She's probably in that Mrs. Harper's office right now, signing me out! Ten o'clock tonight, I'll be sitting on Shirley's front steps, smoking a cigarette and watching car lights as they stripe past the house and down the street. I can *feel* the night air on my face.

But until my mother comes to get me, while I'm stuck here in review, at least I know I'm safe. I won't get stood up, because I've been doing everything they want. So everything's fine. I'm fine. Right?

"You need to stop looking at the girl sitting next to you and start looking at your own F.O.S. list! Being full of shit is gonna keep you in a world of hurt. And this group *always* knows when you're F.O.S.!"

It's Barrette Chick. The original ugly, from my intake. She won the prize. She gets to scream at me first tonight because she motivated so hard, she was practically turning cartwheels on the side of group. Now she's zigzagging through the chairs. She's done with me, and everyone else is churning for their chance. But I still smell her trashcan-breath rising from the wet she left on my face, from her spit therapy.

Scratchy Lip is next. She's the new group hero, 'cause she "revealed herself." Now she's revealing her tonsils to me. Her bag boobs are jamming into my front. Even with slapped back bangs, this girl's tough.

"We know what you're thinking. We all had the same stupid fantasy. Somebody's coming to save you, right, *Cyndy*? You think your druggie boyfriend's going to break our doors down to get some more of your nasty blow jobs. And until your scummy savior gets here, you can get us off your back by 'playing good,' by saying a rule in rules rap. Sound about right?"

She's getting louder as she goes. "Well guess what? Nobody rescued me, and they ain't coming for you, either! If someone was coming for your ass, where the fuck are they? This group *is* your savior, little girl! You're trapped here. Now get used to it!"

She sits down so hard her chair shrieks, but Scratchy's grinning. Grinning and spinning her arms up over her head. Her "Love ya!" from the girls' side is extra, extra huge.

I'm picturing my mother, a hundred feet away from me in that carpeted room. It's gonna feel so good to hug her when she comes to withdraw me! If she'd just come through that door and see what they're doing to me, she'd—she'd—she'd stand there, like she did in the bathroom when Jacque was all over me. She'd stand there and watch.

A fist punches my head and shakes the truth loose. Scratchy is right. My mother's not gonna come save me. And if my own mother doesn't care, why the fuck would my "druggie friends" care? They didn't try to see me when I was right there in Bridgeport, at Janus House. Like they're gonna come bust down some warehouse walls in Virginia? Quit dreamin', stupid! Joanna's not thinking about me, and neither is Steve. They don't give a fuck. Nobody does.

This place is my cage.

I'm not leaving tonight. Or next week. Or any time soon. It's just me here. Me and God and the group. If I'm gonna survive, I better start praying a lot harder to one of them.

24

F.O.S. LISTS GO THROUGH A FIFTH-PHASER, UP THE CHAIN OF COMMAND, TO EXECUTIVE STAFF

It's Tuesday morning, and Scott's smiling. And when staff's in a good mood, group's in a good mood. "Y'all!" Scott yells. "How much do you trust your group?"

That's a good question. You can do a lot with that. You can prove that you forgive the group, even after review last night. You can make them like you, so they don't ever stand you up in review again. Yeah. This one's mine. I'm gonna get this. My snapping hands are up before anyone else's.

"Cyndy Etler!" Scott says, and I pop to my feet. "You're on fire today! I like it. What can you tell us, to prove your trust?"

Waves of electricity roll through me. This thing I'm about to say? The only other person who knows about this is Jacque. But fuck it. "I have a beauty mark, right on the middle of my left boob!" I say. Actually, I kind of yell.

And oh my God, they cheer. They laugh and they cheer.

They laugh and they cheer and they motivate to be next up. It worked. The group likes me. I'm safe. Here we go.

Next is a boy, Mike K. "In my druggie past, when I was six, my seventeen-year-old druggie friend made me put his dick in my mouth. He told me to pretend it was a lollipop." We laugh at that one too. Some guy claps and yells, "Love ya, Lolli!" Damn. Today's fun.

Scott's looking at the kid in the bull's-eye seat on the guys' side. That kid's been in the bull's-eye since I got here. I noticed him my first day, and even though now I know not to look at the boys' side, I know he's still sat there every day. First seat, front row.

"Ty Smith!" Scott says to him. The kid doesn't stand, but Scott keeps smiling. "Ty, you ready to get honest? You ready to trust this group?"

Ty doesn't move. He doesn't look like he *can* move. He's sitting up so he doesn't get his spine punched, but otherwise, he looks dead. Eyes down, lids halfway closed, mouth open.

"Stand up!" Scott yells in his ear. Ty doesn't even flinch. "Stand his ass up," Scott says, and two fifth-phasers are **BOOM** right behind Ty, with their hands wedged tight in his armpits. When they lift him, Ty doesn't move a muscle to help. You can tell.

Scott's still smiling as he stands in front of dead-eye Ty. The fifth-phasers are struggling to hold him up. "Ty! *Amigo!* What drugs have you done?" Scott asks.

"Pot and alcohol," Ty says.

"What drugs have you done?" Scott repeats.

"Pot and alcohol."

"Bullshit. What drugs have you done?"

"Pot and alcohol."

"Who believes him?" Scott smiles at us, and nobody raises a hand. "Who *claimed* they'd only done pot and alcohol, when they were still F.O.S.?" Everybody raises a hand. Both hands. Both fists. "Who thinks Ty needs some help getting honest?" Scott says to the room full of flapping arms. "Who knows what a marathon is?" The fists spin into weapons. "Get him out of here. Take him to a marathon room," Scott tells the fifth-phasers, and they drag the kid away, toward the room where they killed Amanda's eyes.

"Guys' side!" Scott yells, his smile bigger than ever. "Who's up for a marathon?" Holy fuck. It's gonna be a bloodbath. "Pete B.! Joe C.! Go ahead!" Two guys race to the Amanda room. In the second between when they open the door and slam it behind them, boy voices come through like whip cracks.

They keep Ty in there for all of trust rap, all of phaser rap, and all of rules rap. They keep him in there for lunch rap, girls' and guys' rap, and exercise rap. When they're lining us up for dinner, one of the fifth-phasers sprints from the little room back to the staff office, then sprints back with John and a backpack. This time when the door opens, I hear Ty crying. He's saying, "Mommommom." I swear.

At the end of dinner rap, the door opens again. Scott yells

at us, "Eyes up here! Song!" and the group turns forward and motivates. But I know some phasers turn to look back, like they did when I was first brought in. I know because I'm one of them.

The fifth-phasers and John are walking Ty to the back of group. Then they stop, halfway between the girls' side and the guys', and instead of picking a song, Scott yells, "Incoming!" The rest of the group turns around and looks at Ty. We stare at Ty's right hand because it's all wrapped in bandages, big as a balloon.

"Group, this is Ty," John tells us. "Ty is from Dedham, Massachusetts. He went to Dedham High School. The drugs he's done are—Ty, what drugs have you done?"

It's like a rewind to ten hours ago, when Scott first stood him up in group. Ty's eyes are half-shut, and his voice is like a robot with low batteries. But his words are all new. "Pot, alcohol, mushrooms, LSD, cocaine, uppers, and downers."

"Very nice!" Scott says with a sneer. I can't believe I ever thought his John Stamos face looked friendly. "Next thing you know, you'll be doing a whole full o' shit list, Ty! Bet you're gonna write a killer M.I. tonight about getting honest… You left-handed, I hope?"

Ty doesn't answer, but Scott lets it go. When the fifth-phasers bring him back to first seat, front row, Ty raises his balloon-hand to choose a song. It's the first time, I think, he's ever motivated. What happened in that room? What *happens* in that room?

On the ride back to her house, Sandy explains F.O.S. to me. It stands for Full of Shit. She tells me people make F.O.S. lists all the time, as part of their fourth step, "Admit to God, myself, and another human being the exact nature of my wrongs, immediately." Everything they haven't been telling the group, all of the horrible, grody, evil things they've ever done? It all gets written down and sent up to executive staff, to be kept in their file.

You don't get off first phase before you do a F.O.S. list, Sandy says. Usually the first one's not honest enough, and you have to do another, where you tell the *really* bad stuff. She wouldn't tell me what was on hers until we were alarmed in the phaser room, but that made sense. I wouldn't want my mother to hear that I'd had sex with my brother, either. But *man.* No *way.*

"Did you really do that?" I ask.

"I just told you I put it on my F.O.S. list, didn't I?" she says back.

It's an answer, but not to the question I asked.

Now, instead of sleeping, I'm lying on my mattress, counting. If I'm ever gonna get out of Straight, I have to make second phase. Get the hand out of my pants so I can run. And to make second phase, I've have to do a F.O.S. list of all the drugs I've done. Right now, I've only got two: pot and alcohol. Not enough. They don't believe me. I wouldn't, either. How can you be in drug rehab if you've only been drunk once and smoked pot twice? But that's not what matters. A Full of Shit list has to be beefy.

If you think about it, though, this whole fucking Straight thing is crazy. Two months ago I had never done drugs. But I had to *pretend* to smoke pot, so I could fit in in Bridgeport, so I could escape my house. Now I have to pretend I've done *more* than smoke pot, so I can fit in at this warehouse of kids, to get *back* to my house. And fuck am I bad at lying. Plus, I don't even know what drugs are out there, really.

But if *I* don't know, how could anyone else at Straight know, either? We're all just teenagers. How many drugs can you actually fit into fifteen years on earth? And if these kids' lives are like mine... God! Has anyone in here actually *done* drugs?

Man, I have to watch myself. These are the kinds of questions that get you slaughtered. I need to be wicked careful, even of what I think. Because the group can read your mind, obviously. So I can't think about what drugs I *haven't* done. I need to think about what drugs I *could* have done.

When other kids stand up and say the drugs they've used, it's like they're reading from a chart. "I've done pot, alcohol, hash, hash oil, Thai weed, Thai stick..." Those, everybody says. Can I? Well, hash, I've heard the Zarzozas talk about. Maybe there was some in a joint I took a hit off? So, I can say that I've smoked hash. And Thai weed? Well, *weed* is *pot*, and I've smoked pot. What's the difference between *Thai* weed and *pot* weed? None. Okay, so I've smoked Thai weed. Now I've done pot, alcohol, hash, and Thai weed. I'm up to four...what else do kids say they've done? Heroin,

LSD—I don't even know what those are, so I can't say I've done them. Cocaine? No, that song says it's "white lines." I'd know if I'd done something that came in lines.

What about over-the-counter drugs? When I first moved to Monroe, I took a bunch of aspirin one day, then drank this brown stuff I found in the medicine cabinet, kind of hoping it would kill me... Those are over-the-counter drugs, right? And, hey! If I was taking stuff out of the medicine cabinet, probably some of it was prescription drugs, right? I'll add both of those to my list, too, which brings me up to six. So now, I've done six drugs. Awesome. They're gonna love me. Second phase, here I come!

25

NO ASKING PARENTS FOR WANTS AND NEEDS DURING TALK

The group likes us both now, me and Amanda. They're liking me because Sandy stood up in group Wednesday and said, "My newcomer has something to share!"

Then I got up and said, "The drugs I've actually done are pot, alcohol, hash, Thai weed, over the counter drugs, and prescription drugs."

Matt King said to Sandy, "Get it in writing and send it up the chain of command." He said it in a voice like she was stupid or something, but to me, he was really nice. He said, "Nice job, Cyndy. Way to get honest. Love ya."

Love ya! He told me "love ya!" Okay, maybe Matt King *is* as cute as Scott Deutermeyer. Yeah, he is.

They're liking Amanda because she's a totally different person. She motivated and stood up yesterday, and she was finally wearing something other than druggie clothes. It kind of hurt to look at her, though, because Amanda does *not* belong in pleated khakis and pink button downs. Even her skull looked soft. Less than a week in here, and her killer shaved head's become a fuzzy Easter chick.

It was her very first time sharing about her past, and Amanda blew everyone away. I mean, honesty like a twisting knife.

"Boys didn't want to fool around with me," she said. She did the Vanna White, sweeping her hand from her boobs to her knees, like, *See why?* "So I became a boy."

Now that's some complicated shit. I've been thinking about it ever since. Amanda became a boy? Really? I mean, so, she dressed like a boy, and got big like a boy. She shaved her head like a boy. But she didn't *become* a boy—she's still got her z-z, right? She has to! I can see Amanda naked in my head, with arms that look like thighs, and thighs that look like hams. Layers of belly curl down over her hips. But you know something? I bet when you've got that much flesh smooshed around your z-z, it feels really safe. Like you might as well not even have one.

I don't know if this is going to make sense to you. I don't even know if it makes sense to me. But twelve hours in group every day has given me a lot of time to think, and I've started kinda figuring stuff out. Like when I was younger, Jacque would hit me all the time. And he would do stuff to me with Vaseline. And that was okay with my mother, and I was too young to do anything about it.

But then we moved to Monroe, and I turned old enough to fight. That's when I hid my z-z, and that's when Jacque started chasing me, beating on doors to get to me. And that, for some reason, was *not* okay with my mother.

Does any of that make sense? Like, maybe I made the house too loud. Or my mother didn't want me to make her lose her husband. Maybe she couldn't stand me getting the attention, not her. Whatever it was, she had to fix the problem. So she locked me up in this place. Not for *me*, but for *her*.

Hey, *that's* what I can share with the group! They'll finally understand! I don't have a drug problem, I have a mother problem. Everyone will feel bad for me, and they'll *make* my mother sign me out. I just have to tell them the truth.

I get myself called on with this motivating trick I learned. You go hard while doing this sideways-snapping with your fingers. I'd try to explain how to do it, but it wouldn't work. You've never been in group yourself, watching how the oldcomers motivate, and that's the only way to learn it. So, sorry.

Scott's leading a family rap, which is perfect, because he's actually met Jacque. Kim must have told Scott how evil Jacque is, at least a little bit. I mean, Kim hasn't, like, been on the bathroom floor with Jacque, but she's definitely seen him hit me. So Scott will *totally* be able to picture what I'm talking about. He'll totally get it.

My special snap makes Scott pick me first. I'm standing

here smiling at him and the group because this is my moment. I'm going to tell. Finally, somebody who will listen to what really happened! They're going to care. They'll apologize for spitting on me, and they'll wish me luck as I walk out the door.

"This was a month and a half ago," I tell them. "It was a Thursday night, exactly two weeks before my fourteenth birthday. I was getting my clothes out of the dryer, to pack to go to Bridge—to my druggie friend's for the weekend."

The group is looking at me, every single kid. Nobody's motivating; nobody's trying to spit in my face. They're just…listening. It feels like a warm bubble bath.

"So my mother's hus—I mean, my stepfather heard me open the dryer, and he ran at me. And I ran too, but I ran the wrong way. I ran into the bathroom. I trapped myself."

As I'm telling the story, I'm back there. I'm feeling it happen, way more than I did when it actually happened. The cold toilet edge digs into my leg; the walls box me into place. The heat of my tears, the hate of my voice, the rip of his fist. The fight for who gets control of my z-z. Him or me. And the nothing, the *nothing*, of my mother.

I don't know what my words are, exactly, but I'm telling them what happened in the Monroe bathroom that night. And when I was little, in the Stamford bathroom, with Vaseline. I'm standing here in this mongoloid warehouse room, sobbing. I haven't told anyone what Jacque does to me. And now I'm telling hundreds of people, girls *and* boys.

I look up at Scott and he's looking back at me, that same priest-sweet way he did when I first got here.

"Done?" he asks.

I nod and collapse, my hands all over my face. And my group lifts me up with a "LOVE YA, CYNDY!"—so huge, it starts to fix me. They were with me just now in the bathroom. They understand what happened to me, and they *love* me. They all just said so. This is like, my do-over. That was the past. I got it out, and they understand, and they love me. And now, I'm okay.

The *whish* of my arms is drying my tears as I go *hard,* motivating. Every cell in my body knows that I'm swishing myself up and out. Out of those bathrooms, and out of this place. Any second now I'll be flying. Watch.

26

NO TALKING OUT TO PARENTS IN OPEN MEETING EXCEPT FOR SAYING "I LOVE YOU"

Because it's Friday night, our blood is moving fast through our veins. Friday night means getting to report concerns on people. And showing your parents, in open meeting, how much you've changed. And getting in people's faces in review. You know that lightning ball that zips through your fingers when you break a thermometer? That's what we've got for blood.

The fever got *really* hot in open meeting. Because I got honest with my drug list, I was chosen to do my introduction. And let me tell you, standing there in my big velour pants and my Chico shirt, booming through a microphone that "I'm Cyndy, I'm fourteen, and I *do* believe I'm a druggie!" felt great. Even though I *don't* believe that, saying what they want me to feels great. Like joining a big club, taking a blood oath with my group.

Now we are One. Forever.

When my mother got the mic after my introduction, it set the room on fire. She stood up, her and my—my stepfather—and she cried, "My daughter's back!"

I swelled with pride like that blueberry girl in Willy Wonka, because I knew exactly what my mother was saying: staff *told* her I don't belong in here. She's signing me out tonight! I screamed right back at her.

"LOVE YA, MOM! LOVE YA, DAD!"

And then everyone got the fever. Me, the group, the parents—we were exploding with it.

That was three hours ago. Now they're pulling the wall closed again, blocking our view of our parents. I'm doing a really good job of not turning around to find my mother in the crowd, because no eye games with parents. Instead, I put my hand up in a C above my lap.

Even though I put in for talk, and I think I earned talk, I got nothing again tonight. But why should I care? In four more hours, I'll be ancient history! Besides, I'm getting back at Sandy for saying I deserve nothing on my progress report. I'm putting in a concern on her. It's perfect. I don't even know how I came up with it.

The fifth-phaser's squeezing herself in next to me, and I'm leaning close to her face, and it feels *better* than a stupid talk would've, anyway. It feels like it's just her and me, on the right side, together.

"I have a concern about my oldcomer," I breathe into her ear, behind the wall of my fingers. "It's Sandy G.?"

"Okay," she breathes back.

She tips her pencil over her pad.

"She talked behind backs to me."

"She *did*?"

The fifth-phaser's face is a millimeter from mine. Her eyes are big as clocks.

"Yeah, she did. She talked behind backs about one of the newcomers she had, before me. She said the newcomer had gotten honest in her M.I.—the M.I. was about how she'd had sex with her brother before Straight—but Sandy never reported it."

"Oh, my God. This is like a *double* concern: she talked behind backs *and* she didn't report her newcomer's F.O.S. up the chain of command. This is really good, Cyndy."

The fifth-phaser's words make me feel perfect.

"Great job, Cyndy," she says again. She's, like, the sun and the rain as she pats me on the shoulder before standing and moving away.

And my arms are up, and I'm punching air like a prizefighter. God, does this feel right. I'm leaving this place on a high.

The accordion wall is zipping partway open, letting back in the flood of talkers. Because we want the parents to hear happy, singing druggies, we're doing a new song: "Little Bunny Foo Foo." I don't know this one yet, so I'm just moving my mouth, listening and watching as the group goes nuts.

Little bunny FOO FOO!

Peace signs fly up behind heads to make ears. Fingers curl down twice for Foo Foo.

Hoppin' through the FO-REST!

Fists go pounding down thighs.

Scoopin' up the FIELD MICE!

Hands scoop the air above thighs.

And BOPPIN' 'em on the HEAD!

Now everybody's really having a blast, taking their scoop-shaped right hand and *banging* it over their left fist. I mean, *BAM!*

The words are pretty simple, so I sing it with them the next time around. And I get it. The smacking ourselves. It feels. Fucking. *Great.* We sing it four more times and I'm screaming, loud as anyone. I'm a part of this group! We're alive! And we're gonna *do* something tonight! Let's fucking go!

We motivate like crazy to choose our next song, but someone behind the group is going even crazier. His finger snapping and *gzsh*ing noises are so loud, we all drop our hands and turn and look back at him. It's this fifth-phaser, except he's on a setback. He's belt looped by an oldcomer, being walked back from his talk. And even though we all stopped motivating, he's still going, jumping three feet off the ground. The oldcomer's hand goes along for the ride in his pants.

I turn back to the barstools and see Lucy and Matt King wearing Skeletor grins. Matt does the tiniest finger flick, right to left, and the accordion wall is rumbled shut so fast, I duck my head. The second the latch clicks, *Bang!* Matt calls on the kid.

"John P.!"

John P. drags the oldcomer behind him as he roils toward the girls' side, toward my sun-and-rain fifth-phaser. Who's also his sister. She's frozen at the edge of the chairs, but the other fifth-phasers aren't. They move out and around her, a teenage barricade between her and the guarded doors. Three minutes ago she was taking my concern; now she's practically got a hand in her pants. With the flick of a finger, she dropped from the top to the bottom.

Her brother doesn't speak. He sprays. "I knew it! I heard it said in fifth-phasers/staff rap that you were needed for one-on-one, and I knew it wasn't related to group! I *knew* there were inappropriate feelings! And now our parents tell me that while I've been on setback, you've *talked* on the *phone*? I cannot believe how full of shit you are!"

She's not the sun anymore. She's not the rain. She's an unwatered plant, shriveled and dying. Because of no talking behind backs, I can't understand exactly what her brother is saying she did. But I can tell she did it. Whatever he's accusing her of, she's totally guilty. I throw my hands up and motivate because I'm so mad—I trusted her! She's a fifth-phaser! We're gonna get 'er!

Sam Lancer grabs her by the belt loop and starts dragging her toward the bull's-eye. Another fifth-phaser is taking the concern notebook and pencil from her hand. The group is going nuts, and Matt King is laughing.

"Stop!" he shouts.

We put our hands down and watch as he slowly, *sloooowly* walks over to the girl, dragging his eyes up and down her body as he moves.

"So," he goes. "You got a crush on staff?"

The whole group gasps—you can hear it. It's the same sound as when you vacuum up your mother's best earring. **Fww-uck!** Matt's so close now, he could do spit therapy. But instead, he gets quieter. We all stretch forward to hear what he's saying.

"And not only did you get a crush on staff, but you get a crush on staff that *slips*? On staff that's goin' *back* to drinkin' and druggin'?"

John P. is motivating again, and so are some other kids, including me. Oh my *God*, we're gonna *get* 'er! This is the best concern we've ever—but Matt just keeps going.

"And *then!* You *talk* to druggie *staff* on the *phone*?!"

The group is an earthquake. Nothing, nobody is still.

Except my fifth-phaser. She's so still, she's not breathing. She's in shock. I know because that's how I was last Friday, in my first review. But this time, the beast isn't after me. This time, I'm *part of* the beast. This time is actually fun.

"Nah, put yer hands down," Matt says.

He says it wicked quiet, but somehow we all hear him. And we all obey.

"You know what you did," he says to the girl who used to be a fifth-phaser. "You don't need this group to tell you." Still standing three inches in front of her, he looks over at her brother. "Nice work." He does that same finger flick, but this time, it's left to right. "Get back on the side of group. Yer setback's over."

Then he looks back at her, searching for the best spot for the knife. "How long you been on your phases?"

"Twenty-one months," she tells her shoes.

"Twenty-one months! And you didn't know not to talk to druggie staff on the phone? After twenty-one months? *Good*ness! I bet even a spanking-new newcomer knows better than that!"

Nodding my head yes, I lift my arms up to agree with him, but Matt shakes his head at me, his eyebrows mean. My stomach flips. Okay, no motivating when staff's talking.

"Twenty-one months. And on staff's list for seventh-stepping next week! You were one week away from being *out* of here. Dang. Smooth move, ex-lax. You're started over. Day one newcomer. Hope that phone call was worth it. Have a seat."

She's slammed down into the bull's-eye with the longest, meanest "Looooooove ya!" ever. And we, the group, the beast, we go psycho. We smelled blood, and now we want more.

The boys' and girls' sides never got sent to our separate corners, so I'm seeing how the guys bust ass. They're *sick*!

One tall, skinny kid is motivating with his head leaned back and his chest pushed out, like a foxy momma jutting her tits so you'll notice them. Another dude has his right fist plunging in a Nazi salute while his left fist whips in a circle. His teeth are clenched in a grid; he's in glorious pain. Since you've never been in group, you wouldn't understand it. But we do. *We* do.

Both sides of group are ballistic now. The whole room is raging. And Lucy and Matt are sitting, dead calm, on the barstools. They're cool as Moses, walking through the raging Red Sea. Then Lucy lifts a hand and snaps her fingers. And we all drop. Done. Silent.

"We're gonna do something new tonight, gang. Y'all are so fired up, it's gonna be a co-ed review. So what're you waiting for? Go ahead! Bust yer asses! Who wants to talk to this group?"

Raaaaaahhhhrrrr! we scream back at her, but not with our mouths. We scream with our arms, our legs, our fingers, our bellies, our hair. People are spinning up out of their seats and balancing in thin air, with their knees just *barely* bent, so they're not *officially* standing up with nobody holding their belt loop. They churn the air with their fists for a split second before *crash*, gravity wins, and their tailbone meets blue plastic. Chairs are coming unlinked and the floor tiles are a Slip'N Slide of sweat.

"You guys are *lame!*" Lucy screams. "*Lame!* We had to wheel out garbage barrels for phasers' *puke* during bust-ass raps in St. Pete. But you guys aren't even breathing heavy! What a bunch of fucking pussies!"

We crank the volume hard, to prove that we're no pussies. I'm a human jackhammer, begging to be called on, to shoot to my feet and *howl.* To throw my head back and rip my throat open and scream out the hell, the power, the *thank you!* to this group for making me feel so good. So strong. So *part* of something. I've never felt so much a *part.*

That's when I have my very first punch. My virgin fucking punch. I'm spinning my fists over my head when *crack!* My fist is kicked back, hard, by someone's skull.

Oooooh! Fuck you, I'm gonna getcha!

Plugged in, mega-volt, I thwack. Every and any arm, chest, or head that's around me, I crack it with my fists. And I get cracked. And I slip in our cocktail of floor sweat. I bang down onto my kneecaps, and jerk back into my seat. I thwack and I plunge and I crack.

A boy is stood up and blasted for being a whiny baby during exercise rap. He gets diaper therapy. He'll have to wear giant Pampers in group, nothing else. A girl is stood up for wasting her host home's shampoo and toothpaste. She gets T.P. therapy. Her oldcomer will hand her three squares when she poops, and that's all the T.P. she'll get.

And it's good, it's good, it's good. We're motivating, tasting each other's blood, and it's so good. Because when you're busting ass, you're flying. You're strong, you're safe. When another kid gets blasted, it's not you. We're busting our asses for Matt and Lucy and we're gonna *get* 'em, *someone*, whoever gets stood up next. The sweat and the spit are flinging off our teeth and nails and—

"*Cyndy Etlerrrrrr*!"

—and my stomach drops, like the earth disappeared from underneath me. Like I'm in that carnival ride, that giant tube you press your back against and it starts spinning, harder and faster, and the floor drops away and you spinspinspin hardfasthard and you're pancaked on the wall and there's no floor underneath you and you scream and you scream and you scream but there's no mommy.

I stand.

"Why'd your father touch you, Cyndy?"

Lucy's wearing her Satan smile.

"Whaddaya mean? I mean—"

The walls and the hands, everything is spinning around me.

"What did you do, Cyndy?" Lucy jabs.

"I—I mean, I closed my eyes, and I talked to God. I—"

"What'd she do, group?"

Raaahhrr! goes the beast.

The Nazi salute guy jumps up. "You little shit!" he goes, shoving boy-chairs out of his way. Oh my God, he's coming to the girls' side! He's coming to get me! He's so close, he could be kissing me, but he's not. He's screaming in my face.

"I couldn't *wait* to call you out when you were whining! What did you do to make your father bring you to that bathroom? What flirty shit did you do to make him get the Vaseline? Or should we *guess*? A full of shit druggie slut like you—"

Lucy cuts him off. "Okay, back to the boys' side! Thank you! Neeeeeext!"

Next is my demoted fifth-phaser. She loved me for my concern, now she's screaming at me from the bull's-eye.

"This isn't about your parents! This is about *you*! Whatever he did, you brought it on yourself! Just like I did, to get this setback! You really think you can fool this group?"

"*Thank* you, newcomer," Scott cuts her off. "Cyndy, I hope you heard what she said. You're never going to get anywhere with this group while you're blaming everyone else. You better get honest—not only with your drug list, but with your*self*."

But I—but I *got* honest. I can't get any *more* honest. What else do they want me to do?

I thought I asked that out loud, but Lucy doesn't hear me. She picks up where Scott left off.

"You can relate again when you're being honest. 'Til then, have a seat."

Lucy's words are like Joanna's doorbell. They go from high to low, with a period after each one.

Have.

A.

Seat.

It's the fall of the guillotine, a death sentence. A short, hard shove off the edge of the world.

NOVEMBER 1985

DECEMBER 1985

JANUARY 1986

FEBRUARY 1986

MARCH 1986

APRIL 1986

MAY 1986

JUNE 1986

JULY 1986

AUGUST 1986

SEPTEMBER 1986

OCTOBER 1986

NOVEMBER 1986

DECEMBER 1986

JANUARY 1987

FEBRUARY 1987

MARCH 1987

27

NO *SATURDAY NIGHT LIVE* OR 98 ROCK FM

It never feels right when I have to be here in the front office, sitting in actual sunlight with the runner badge on. God. For the past sixteen months I've basically only seen those few seconds of sunlight a day, racing from the car to the building. By the time we leave, it's dark out again.

I have to turn away when someone opens the smoked-glass office doors, because the world on the other side of them is terrifying. Cars and people and buses and a trillion other things that could take you *straight* back to drinking and drugging. And they all blaze like flashing DANGER signs in the light of the sun. At least it's winter sun. How am I gonna deal in, like, June?

But I can't think about that. By June, they will have seven-stepped me. So I won't be a Straightling anymore; I'll be a Straight "graduate." But like...leaving Straight, and living back at my mother's house? Not reporting to the building every day? Going back to my druggie *high* school? No way. I can't even *think* it. I will freak right out.

I'll think about the date, instead. It's March. March 27, 1987. The runner has to always know the date. What if executive staff asked me the date for somebody's intake paperwork? March 27, '87. March 27, '87.

That's a good head-chant too. I can use it instead of the *Odd Couple* song. I guess non-Straightlings don't need a head-chant, 'cause they don't need to block druggie music from their thoughts. Or if they do, they haven't gotten honest with themselves about it yet. For me, though, when I'm not in group, I have to sing the *Odd Couple* song in my head non-stop. I'm such a druggie that if I didn't, all my druggie music would take back over my mind. I've tried and tried to let go of it, but still. The second I quit my head-chant, the druggie music comes right back.

I don't need a head-chant when I'm in group, though. When I'm in rap sessions, listening to other Straightlings share about their past, I'm safe. Group is the only place the world feels right, which is why I only leave when they make me be runner. But staff has been doing that a lot lately. They say, "You need to get comfortable away from group. Here, put on the badge. You're afternoon runner."

Which is scary as hell, because the only time staff wants us comfortable outside group is if we're about to be seven-stepped. But who ever heard of a sixteen-month program?! Nobody's ready to seven-step after only sixteen months!

You haven't felt the safety, the—God, just the perfection, the *right*ness of group. So you wouldn't understand. But I do. Once I got honest with myself and realized I'm a total druggie and alcoholic, everything about Straight, Inc. made sense. Outsiders don't have to get it, because we do. That's all that matters.

An addict is an addict is an addict. Before I had done a single drug, I jumped into smoking cigarettes. The first time I smoked? I bought a whole pack. Know what that is? Proof. Proof that I'm an addict.

And cigarettes lead to pot, which leads to coke, which leads to shooting up. It doesn't matter that I didn't actually do coke. I would have, if you'd put it in front of me. It's only by the grace of God, and my mother putting me in Straight, that I didn't have to sink that far to hit bottom. And it wasn't just me that I hurt! If Straight hadn't been here for me, I would've destroyed my whole family. Now, thanks to the group, I understand that.

My sobriety is going to be *so* challenged when they make me leave here! Connecticut is a *long* way from the building, and I guarantee you, there are zero Straightlings in Monroe. Monroe may as well be on Jupiter. Plus, I'll be in the exact same house where I lived when I started drinking and drugging. I'll be sleeping in the same *bed*. If I don't have group to go share with, what am I supposed to do with all of those memories?

I've been back to that house two times, for my fifth-phase weekend passes. And it was *horrible*. Horr-i-*ble*. Like on my first visit, I had to call the building to report myself for being in the house at the same time as alcohol. Can you believe it?! My father had alcohol in the house. Fucking alcohol! In the house! And then on my second visit, I had to call in *again* because they gave catnip to Kitty for Christmas. *Totally* an addictive substance, right? But—but staff *laughed* at me when I called! Like, it's okay for me to enable my druggie cat?!

And then my mother made me sit in the car while she drove by fucking Masuk. I was like, "Hello, my druggie fucking high school?! I'm a fucking phaser! You can't expose me to the biggest threat to my sobriety like that!"

She didn't even care. She was just like, "This will be great practice for you, for when you come home and face reality." Then, when we got back to the house, she made me clean the puke off her car's floor mat. But what am I going to do when I have to go *in* my druggie high school? That day, it won't be just puke. When I have to actually go *in* Masuk? My fucking head will explode. And where am I supposed to put the chunks of shattered brain?

No! I have to stop this! I can't even think about that house, that school. I have to think about how to squeeze myself through the carpet room without touching any boy siblings. That's where they keep all the families before open meet—hey, that's not—*no*. No *way*! That kid can't be my stepbrother! He's *never* been to the building. But—it *is* him! He's right next to my mother, with her gross smug "That's *my* daughter" smile on. And they're both all dressed up!

Do you know what this means? It means—*fuck!* They're seven-stepping me in open meeting tonight! It means I have to go to bed in my old druggie bedroom tomorrow night, and the next night, and every other night from now on. It means no locks on the windows and no alarms on the doors. It means no group to report to in the morning. It means nothing—*nothing*—to keep me safe. It means I'm fucking *fucked*.

28

NO NEWCOMERS WEAR BELTS

Holy shit. My druggie high school is *big*. Big and fucking scary. Nobody gave me a bucket or sponge, so now every day when I get off the bus and come through Masuk's front doors, I have to walk past my brain bits, splattered all over the brick entrance walls.

My first few days back were a nightmare. They were like review on fucking steroids. But now that it's been a week, the actual time in class is almost kind of becoming okay, because I just have to sit and listen to the teacher and not look at anybody. As long as we don't have to choose partners for a project, I can semi-deal. But in the halls between classes? Jesus. Gimme the choice, and I'll choose hell.

Lunch is even worse, because everybody's there and they're all sitting still, looking for somebody to talk about. It's not like I can go hide in the bathroom, the way I did in middle school. Even if I wasn't terrified of walking in on somebody snorting coke, everybody would *know* I was going in there to try to hide. Because they're all, always, watching me. I'm Cyndy Etler, the girl who rocked hard for a sec, then vanished...and reappeared, a year and a half later, as a deaf mute. Nobody can take their eyes off me.

And did I ever tell you about the giant windows that separate the cafeteria from the smoking pit? Yeah. *Giant.* So every time I set foot in the caf, the whole fucking pit's watching me, too. All my old druggie friends. And listen, you better not tell my seven-step group this, but...I miss them. I *really* miss them.

My first day back at Masuk though? That was the *absolute* worst. It's just three friggin' days after I seven-step, right? So all I want is to be back in group. There's nobody in the hallways of Masuk yelling *Love ya, Cyndy!* Believe me. So my first day back I'm scurrying down the hall to Spanish class, but you'd think I'm wearing a strobe light, the way everyone's staring. My chin is, like, bruising my chest bone, it's pointed down so hard. And out of nowhere there's this **tap-tap-tap** on my shoulder. Total flashback to my freshman year, on the gym bleachers, when I met Jo—I mean, when I met my best druggie friend. That day when I turned around and there she was, smiling that half-smile and saying, "Nice shirt. You like the Stones?"

Tap-tap-tap again. "Cynd!"

So I turn, and there she is. Joanna. The only person ever

who was mine, all mine. She liked me best out of everyone, same as I liked her. Her hair is a rock-star mane around her big half-smile.

"I can't believe it's you!" she says. "God! Where the fuck've you *been?* It's been, fucking, two years! Why the fuck didn't you call me?"

It all comes back in a tidal wave, everything Jo gave me. I was trapped in a sewer before I met Jo, but she wrenched the cover off; she showed me the stars and the sky. She taught me cool is *being* cool, not trying to be, and free is *being* free, not wanting to be.

And she—she missed me. She's mad I didn't call her! So that whole time I was in group, she was out here thinking about me? She's been in Bridgeport every weekend all this time, wondering where I *am*? She thinks I could've *called* her?! But I—I mean, she—she has no idea! If I'd known she wanted me there with her, I would have—fucking, *druggie thoughts!* What the fuck am I thinking? I can't—

"Fuckin' Etler, man!" she says, the most beautiful words in the world. Her arms are stretched out to hug me, and she smells like night and Marlboros. She's still *exactly* who she was when I left. She's still Joanna.

But me? I'm not "still" anything. I'm a Straightling.

"It's not in my best interest to talk to you," I tell her.

Her arms drop to her sides. She stares at me, but I can't look back. If I do, the tidal wave—of Bridgeport, of nights out walking, of feeling like I *have* someone—could drown me. Jo's quiet for a second, then she turns and walks away. I know it by the scuff of her work boots. It's the saddest sound in the world.

Staff warned me this moment would happen. Thank God they told me exactly what to say when it did. What staff didn't warn me about was my nosy guidance counselor. I'm already a circus freak in my plaid dress, a hand-me-down from my mother. This panting counselor—ripping into science class, interrupting the teacher, and rasping out my name—she doesn't help my cause.

She pats my head the whole walk to her office, like I'm a giant injured bird. That's before she introduces herself as the new "adolescent addictions specialist." When she leans forward for our heart-to-heart, I see myself reflected in her glasses. I look like a trophy, not a teen.

"Cyndy," she says, "you need to be strong. You're our one clean and sober student."

I'm like, *lady!* You think I don't know this?

Then she traps me. "I was in the cafeteria line when I heard your name. Naturally, I stepped closer. It was a curly-haired girl in a denim jacket talking to a dark-haired girl who I believe might be one of the Beacon Falls students. Do you know these girls?"

I nod. She's lucky I even say that much.

"I had to pull you out of class, so you would know what's going on. We're going to keep you safe. But promise me you'll be strong in your sobriety."

Now what the fuck is *this*? What's that part of the Bible where God keeps raining hell on some poor guy, to test his faith? That guy's name is Cyndy.

But she doesn't understand how much Straight taught me. There is no *chance* I'm going back to drinking and drugging; I would kill myself first. And Jesus! Is it her sobriety or mine? Some seconds tick past, enough to count as a promise. Then, right before I freak out on her, she starts up again.

"She was very upset, the girl in the denim jacket. The one who used your name. That must be why she said what she did. So I want you to—"

Holy shit, I can't take any more. "*What did Joanna say?*" I say. I mean, I *snap*. Like, at a grown-up. If I was in group right now, I'd get pulverized.

My counselor's eyes go all wide and her mouth crimps tight in a pucker, but I don't look away, which gives her no choice but to answer me.

"She said, 'I'm gonna kick Cyndy Etler's ass.'"

Suddenly I realize I need *tons* of after school tutoring from my teachers, to get caught up and all. Because I am *not* being the new Kara Anderson, getting her head slammed in front of the whole bus line. I don't care if I have to walk the five miles back to my mother's house.

So here's an important lesson. When you're a Straightling back at your druggie high school, if you want to not die of shame and weirdness, you need at *least* one friend to eat lunch with. I got smart and dug out my elementary school flute, and now, instead of hanging with Joanna, I'm trying to be friends with the band kids. The ones who are in youth group at church. They're friends with God too, so you'd think they'd be okay. But even they don't get me. They don't get the rules.

Like the other day. It's one of those horrible, like, "social free times" when the band teacher says we can "just hang out 'til the bell rings." So I'm sitting with them and trying to be normal when Denise says she's gonna tell her parents she's staying at Robin's so she can go to a keg party at John's.

Of course, I'm like, "But…you can't go to an alcohol party—you're only fifteen! And you can't lie to your parents, can you?" I tell her that if she does, I'll have to report her.

And she goes, "You have to *what*?"

They all totally laugh at me. The mean way. Oh my *God*, if I could get Denise stood up in review, my group would fucking *kill* her.

I picture the group's faces, their motivating arms, as I stand up and walk out of band. I feel their slapping skin and *kzsh*-ing spit as it hits me, all the way to the girls' room. I hear their *love ya, Cyndy* as I race past the staring lip gloss mirror girls and slam-lock the door to the handicap stall. I keep my group with me—seeing them, feeling them, hearing them—as I hide in that stall for the next five hours. And I don't care who friggin' knows it.

I might have to start hiding in the bathroom at home too. From Jacque. My mother's divorcing him. She's totally grateful to Straight because all the parent meetings on how to deal with your druggie kid taught her that there was a whole other alcoholic making her life shitty: her husband. She got the balls to kick him out, so now I don't have to say I love him anymore.

But I can't feel too safe, because it's not like he forgot where he used to live. He could show up at the house any time. Like Saturday. I'm in Kim's room, doing her Jane Fonda exercise tape. It makes me really sweaty, so I'm exercising next to the open window. And since I'm home alone, I'm wearing just a bra and short shorts. The shorts are in the trash can now with like, a shit stain up the back.

After the leg lifts, at the end of Michael Jackson's *mamasay-mamasah-mama-kusah* song, the tape goes quiet, and I hear this **TINK** right above my head. I stand up to look out the open lower window and there he is, *right* underneath it. Staring up at me with little flames in his eyes. My gut drops straight to China.

He raises his fist, and even his *fist* is mad and red. "Openah door, Cinny!" he shouts, and I'm jerked back to two years ago, crunched in the corner of my room. I'm staring at my bedroom door, praying it stays locked, and hating myself for crying. It's like no time has passed. Nothing has changed. I'm trapped.

"*Openah door!*"

There's only a screen and six feet of air between us, and he's *pissed* that he can't get in. He's here to pick up my baby half-sister. It's his visitation weekend, but my mother took my sister out, and must have forgotten to warn me he was coming. Thank God I always double-lock the front door, now that there's no host-parent to alarm and lock me in.

He throws another rock at the top half of the window. A big one. It doesn't **TINK**, it **CRACK**s. A spider of glass crawls out from the spot where it hit.

"They're not here!" I yell down from where I'm standing, wrapped in the curtain like a robe. I can't move, or the curtain will fall and he'll see my boobs again. "They're gone!" I yell, like, *hint-hint: you should be gone, too!* But he doesn't move, so I try louder. "They went out! They'll be back later!"

That makes him even madder. He stands there and flames, then throws another handful of pebbles at me. Finally, he gets in his car and leaves. But that doesn't mean he won't be back. And what if one time I forget to lock the door?

Sometimes—okay, a lot of times—I wish I wasn't around anymore. I just—I don't *work*, out here. The only place for me is back in Straight, but that's not going to happen. They don't let you back in unless you slip, and I am *not* sacrificing Straight's gift, my sobriety. Besides, my mother already told me she's done spending money on me.

But see, there's no place besides Straight where I'm not terrified. Nobody's totally honest, and follows the rules, and knows how drugs and alcohol fuck you up, the way my group does. So other than Straight, the only safe place for me is heaven.

But I'm still thinking about...you know. Doing something like that. If I did it, I'd just turn on my mother's car and close the garage door and close my eyes. Because pills don't actually make you die; they make you puke. Me and all the other phasers learned that in our druggie pasts. And I could never cut myself. But doing it the car way, it would just be like falling asleep. I'd dream I was back in Straight, and I'd feel safe. And soon enough, I'd *be* safe.

There are two things that have made me not do it yet: God and my meetings. It's not that I believe you go to hell if you kill yourself. To me, it seems like God would *extra* love people who were sad enough to kill themselves. But I don't think that's His first choice for me. This is weird, but...I feel like He has some stuff for me to do before I'm gone. I don't know what it is yet, but I get this feeling, sometimes, like it's a math equation.

Things are really hard + Figuring out how to be okay = Helping others be okay too.

So I'm trying to finish the equation, you know? To work out the how-to-be-okay part, so I can do the helping-others-be-okay-too part.

Plus, I don't want to miss any of my Alcoholics Anonymous meetings. They're the closest I come to being back in group. You don't stand up when you share at AA meetings, you talk from your seat. And after you share they say, "Thanks, Cyndy," not "Love ya." So it's not exactly the same. But everyone listens; that's the important part. Even the people who don't turn and look at you while you talk—sometimes they'll nod at what you're saying.

I liked these meetings when I first got to come to them, on my fifth phase weekend passes. They were the only good thing about those trips. But I didn't realize that they're like a half-inch from heaven until the meeting I went to on the night of my first day back at Masuk.

So I'm sitting in one of those folding chairs that only AA meetings have. They're not the clanky, always-cold metal ones. These are plastic chairs that feel all tilty when you move, like they'll tip over if you're not careful. Even though I want to turn sideways to look at my AA group, I have to keep my knees forward as I share about my first day as Masuk's one and only sober student.

"Guidance counseling must be a boring job. She was so psyched to tell me what Jo said, I had to offer her an inhaler."

Laughter floats up around me like helium balloons. Like they get me.

"And when my guidance counselor got to say 'ass' to me—a student—she looked like a dog tasting a pickle. She couldn't believe what was in her mouth."

A few people twist in their chairs to smile at me, risking a cheap-chair topple.

You know what it's like at my AA meetings? It's like being in a room full of good foster parents. They're way older than me, and they have nice smiles and nice eyes and boring sweaters. And I get to have all of them, for the whole hour of the meeting.

Nobody's circling their finger in the air, but I wrap it up anyway. "So that's what tomorrow holds: my best druggie friend's gonna kick my ass. But at least for today, by the grace of God, I'm sixteen months sober."

"Thanks for sharing, Cyndy," the room says.

At the end of the meeting, everyone stands around talking by the table with coffee and cookies. And all these nice grown-ups, all these AA meeting foster parents—they come up to give me a hug. "Glad you're here," they say. "Keep coming."

They *want* me here.

One of these meeting parents is extra special. I met him three months ago, when I was home on my weekend pass. I went to a meeting and sat in the empty chair next to this nice old man. He looked like Santa Claus, minus the beard: seventyish, round pink cheeks, and a belly with his hands folded over it. When I shared how terrified I was of slipping when I seven-stepped, he patted my shoulder. Which kind of freaked me out at first—if someone touches me it means I'm in trouble, right?—but then I looked at him and saw little tears in the corners of his eyes. Like, he doesn't even know me, but he cares *that* much about my sobriety. All the nice grown-ups surrounded *him* after that meeting, not me. Because everybody loves him. His name is Irish Mike.

So now that I'm seven-stepped, and since my mother's too busy, Irish Mike picks me up for meetings in his long maroon car. He drives me back home too. It's two towns out of his way, but he doesn't mind. He says he's "passing it on."

And you're not going to believe this: at the meeting on the night of my first day back, he gave me a seven-step present: a friendship ring! Fourteen-karat gold! It's a heart held up on the sides by two hands. Nobody's ever given me a fourteen-karat gold *anything*. I swear to God it's a message, to help me solve the middle of the math equation. The part where I learn how to be okay.

I *know* I'm gonna work that part out. I'm pretty sure it has to do with how I feel at my AA meetings: like, surrounded by love. Can you even imagine? I mean, these people just met me. Group *said* they loved me the second they saw me, but it took forever for me to *feel*—to feel—well, to feel like I belonged. At the meetings it was instant, and it felt like *love*. And I didn't have to change before they would be nice to me.

But even though the meetings are in church basements, I don't think the love is coming from God. That's the one part of the message I've got figured out. The kind of love that fixes? It comes from random grown-ups, like AA strangers in rickety folding chairs, or maybe a very cool English teacher, or maybe the staff at Janus House. Random grown-ups that take a kid's broken heart and help her fit the pieces back together, and don't want a single thing in return.

So you know what? I don't think I'm gonna do it, that garage thing. I've been praying every night, you know?

Crunching myself into a ball and thanking God for Straight and my AA meetings, and asking what I'm supposed to do. And I think I just figured it out. I think I'm supposed to stick around long enough to become a random grown-up.

Tonight's meeting is over. Me and Irish Mike are walking through the smoking crowd, on our way back to his car. The smoke smells good, like Bridgeport, like Joanna. But it also smells good like tonight, like the AA smokers saying, "'Night, Mike. 'Night, Cyndy. Keep coming back."

Mike stops to talk to someone, so I stop too. I close my eyes and lean my head back and inhale. I inhale as much of that smoke as I can get. Then when I open my eyes, it's like the stars have switched position. Swear to God. It's not the Big Dipper up there, it's a busted heart. With hands on either side of it, pressing it back together. Like it's really possible. Like a heart can get fixed.

Yeah. You know something? I'm gonna be okay. My heart is already starting to heal. And since I'm learning how to fix my heart, I'm gonna help fix other kids' hearts too.

So yeah. I'm gonna be okay. I am. Watch.

EPILOGUE

NO CAMERAS, TAPE RECORDERS, OR RADIOS IN THE BUILDING

Of course, I wasn't a drug addict or an alcoholic. But Straight's job was to convince us we were druggies—and Straight was good at its job. By the time they let me out of Straight, I had a wicked case of Stockholm Syndrome, a psychological flip-flop that can happen in hostage situations.

It works like this: subconsciously, the hostage thinks, "If I can make my captors like me, this whole captivity thing is gonna go a lot better." Even deeper in her subconscious she thinks, "If I can make myself think like my captors, they'll like me even more." So the victim leaves her own mind behind and adopts the mindset of her abusers. She comes to see them as the good guys, as her saviors. When released, a person with Stockholm Syndrome continues to identify with her oppressors, and dreams of being reunited with them. At least, I did.

It was the good grown-ups at the Trumbull, Connecticut AA meetings who put Band-Aids on my psyche after Straight. With no reason to doubt my claims that I was an alcoholic and addict, they welcomed me. They served as my surrogate group. They listened, and they cared. They just cared.

It was school, though, that really saved me. It took me a while to get there. I needed time to figure out how to survive, how to stop hating myself. At twenty-eight, I was right enough in the head to go to college. UMass gave me all kinds of scholarships for being old, poor, and smart. I walked out of there with a 3.97 GPA, academic awards, a couple of degrees, and a whole lot of swagger. Oh, and a career too.

It happened, as the best stuff often does, when I was looking for something else—in this case, a professor's well-hidden office. A bright sign on a concrete wall caught my eye. $15 AN HOUR, it blared. UNDERGRAD TUTORS NEEDED AT DORCHESTER HIGH.

Damn, I thought. For fifteen bucks an hour, I'll do anything. What I didn't know then was that Dorchester was the kind of school with metal detectors at the front door, which was the only door in the building not chained and padlocked. I didn't know that some of the Dot High students worked as prostitutes and small-scale arms dealers, or that I'd be lucky enough to be accepted by them. I didn't know that working with struggling kids would feel like coming home.

At fourteen, inspired by the staff at Janus House, I made a decision to work with kids like me: lost kids, "throwaway" kids. Seventeen years later, I kept that promise to myself when I became a teacher who works, by choice, with the kids society labels "bad."

Because of my horror-show childhood, I get those teens: their wants, their fears, and the fact that they will totally change how they act when they feel respected and inspired to do so. Watching kids change for a living—and I mean really change, so much that even haters see the difference—proves to me that anything is possible.

I once read an article by a physical therapist who worked with burn victims. She focused on the quality of their skin—so tough and yet so glossy, the yin and yang of having walked through fire. In that fire-hardened skin, I saw a metaphor for myself, for all of us former Straightlings who survived, then went on to thrive. If I'd had an easy childhood, I wouldn't have become the rebel I am, always grinning, always grateful. If I hadn't lived through hell, I wouldn't know my current life is heaven; if I hadn't had to fight, I wouldn't know that I've already won. And believe me. Grinning and grateful? It's not a bad way to go through life.

A NOTE FROM THE AUTHOR

Straight, Inc.'s grandfather was a Los Angeles–based cult named Synanon. Founded in 1958, Synanon started out as a drug rehabilitation center for hard-core heroin addicts. There would be no staff at Synanon, no hierarchy. It would just be addicts helping addicts kick their junk. The tools for achieving this goal: isolation, sleep deprivation, and attack therapy. Synonites would scream at, spit on, and humiliate each other during what was called "The Game."

In 1978, a reporter for *Point Reyes Light*, a local newspaper that would go on to win a Pulitzer Prize for its reporting on Synanon, made a strange discovery. Although it was a facility for adults, a large number of children were running away from Synanon. A nearby family had created an underground railroad system to help them escape. A few months later, a grand jury issued a report on Synanon, which included physical and psychological child abuse, as well as the stockpiling of weapons and handguns. In summary, it said that Synanon had changed from a drug rehab facility into a business run by a dictator.[1]

Synanon made its own laws and dealt with its own troublemakers. An ex-member tried to get his young daughter out of the program, and he was beaten into a coma.[2] A lawyer helped a woman win a $300,000 settlement against Synanon, and two Synonites hid a live rattlesnake in the lawyer's mailbox.

When Los Angeles police raided the Synanon facility, they found a tape recording of its founder, Charles Dederich, saying this: "We're not going to mess with the old-time, turn-the-other-cheek religious postures…our religious posture is: don't mess with us. You can get killed dead… I am quite willing to break some lawyer's legs, and next break his wife's legs, and threaten to cut their child's arm off. That is the end of that lawyer. That is a very satisfactory, humane way of transmitting information. I really do want an ear in a glass of alcohol on my desk."

Synanon, which had renamed itself the Church of Synanon (because churches don't have to pay taxes), was shut down after an IRS investigation found it guilty of "financial

1. "Grand Jury Asks Probe of Synanon Allegations," *Register-Guard*, March 13, 1978.
2. Matt Novak, "The Man Who Fought the Synanon Cult and Won," Paleofuture, September 27, 2014.

misdeeds, destruction of evidence, and terrorism." Synanon's legacy—child abuse, investigations by the media and the government, violence against naysayers—would become Straight, Inc.'s DNA.

In 1971, the federal government gave a grant to a Synanon copycat called the Seed, which was founded by a stand-up comic named Art Barker. The Seed's goal was to take Synanon's methods and apply them to child drug addicts…and to children only *suspected* of trying drugs.

Three years later, Congress investigated the Seed and other so-called "behavior modification" programs. The committee was led by political bigwigs: Senator Sam Irvin, who investigated Watergate and brought down President Nixon; Democratic Senator Edward Kennedy of Massachusetts; and Republican Senator Strom Thurmond of South Carolina. The investigation found that these programs were being used for research on how to change human behavior and how to make people comply, and the investigation ultimately found that these experiments were being done on children without parental knowledge or permission. The official report says the treatment model is "similar to the highly refined brainwashing techniques employed by the North Koreans in the 1950s." That would be the Communist North Koreans, who brainwashed their prisoners of war in death camps.

Just like Synanon, the bad press around the Seed led to its closing. But shortly thereafter, a reincarnation of the

Seed popped up, founded by Seed parents.[3] That program was called Straight, Inc. A 1976 *St. Petersburg Times* article described Straight's purpose: "to treat youths between 12 and 18 who have drug-related problems, but are not hard drug addicts."

Two of Straight's founders, Mel and Betty Sembler, explained to *Florida Trend* magazine why they opened the program: their son had smoked weed. As Betty put it, "We saw this as a fundamental breakdown of everything we believe in: family, education, law and order, responsibility to the community. Drugs represented the very antithesis of these values—pure selfishness."[4]

An *Evening Independent* article discussed Straight's medical credentials: "Dr. Leon Sellers, a veterinarian, [is a] founding father of the program." It also described Straight's staff: "six young adults who have experienced drugs and been helped by other treatment programs."[5]

By the late 1970s, Straight, Inc. was a well-known drug treatment center. Self-promotion came easy for Straight; Mel Sembler was a salesman and a real estate tycoon. Before opening youth treatment centers, he sold shopping malls.

The Semblers' political influence also helped boost

---

3. Maia Szalavitz, *Help at Any Cost: How the Troubled-Teen Industry Cons Parents and Hurts Kids* (New York: Riverhead Books, 2006), 23.
4. David Villano, "Money Man," *Florida Trend*, May 1, 1997.
5. Joe Childs, "Straight, Inc. New Drug Program Set for Sept. 1," *The Evening Independent*, July 27, 1976.

Straight's enrollment. As long-time close friends of Republican movers and shakers, Sembler and his wife encouraged First Lady Nancy Reagan to launch an anti-drug movement. Soon afterward, the hugely influential "Just Say No!" campaign was born, and the First Lady and Princess Diana were filmed visiting Straight buildings.

By 1983, Straight was operating two branches in Florida, two branches in Georgia, one in Ohio, and another in Virginia. Claiming to have treated 3,000 drug abusers with a 60 percent success rate, Straight had plans to open twenty-six branches nationwide by 1986.

As Straight was filling new warehouses, the press was reporting on its controversies. In the six months between May and November 1983, seven lawsuits were filed against Straight for physical and mental abuse. A sampling of article titles from the *St. Petersburg Times* reads like a timeline:

> Some Straight Clients Were Illegally Held, State Officials Say
> Girl Forced to Return to a Straight Foster Home, Neighbors Say
> Youth Sues Mother and Drug Treatment Program
> Straight: Six Directors Have Resigned
> Straight Tells Staff Not to Talk

At the center of the controversy stood Dr. Miller Newton, a Straight dad who was hired to join Straight's executive team. He was an ordained minister who had tried twice to get elected to Congress. His doctorate was in public administration and urban anthropology.

In 1982, Florida's state attorney began a major investigation of the program. In that same year, a teen named Karen Norton went through the Straight intake process. Norton would later describe that intake—and the violence done to her that day by Dr. Miller Newton—in a sworn testimony as part of her lawsuit against Straight, Inc. She won the case, to the tune of $722,000.[6]

A year later, the Florida state attorney released their 300-page investigative report. It included eighteen charges of child abuse, including "beatings, sleep deprivation, restricted diets, periods of isolated confinement and physical and mental abuse."[7] Straight was told that if they wanted to keep their license, they would have to stop imprisoning children, withholding food and medical care as punishment, and having teens discipline other teens by sitting on their necks.

Straight didn't deny using these practices. Instead, they said they were working with lawmakers to correct this problem. They corrected the problem by shutting down the Sarasota branch, where the investigation had taken place, and

---

6. Mark Journey, "Straight Client Wins $721,000 Suit," *St. Petersburg Times*, November 10, 1990.
7. Jay Greene, "Straight, Inc. to Shut Down Sarasota Branch," *Bradenton Herald*, July 20, 1983.

IN THE CIRCUIT COURT OF THE SIXTH JUDICIAL CIRCUIT
IN AND FOR PINELLAS COUNTY, STATE OF FLORIDA
CIVIL DIVISION

KAREN NORTON,

Plaintiff,

v.

STRAIGHT, INC.,

Defendant.
_______________/

Case No. 85-11481
Division 15

FL BAR NO. 390674

FINAL JUDGMENT

Pursuant to the jury verdict herein it is,

ORDERED AND ADJUDGED that the Plaintiff, KAREN NORTON, do have and receive of and from the Defendant, STRAIGHT, INC., the sum of $721,000.00, FOR WHICH LET EXECUTION ISSUE.

DONE AND ORDERED in Chambers at St. Petersburg, Pinellas County, Florida, this 9th day of November, 1990.

/S/ Joseph P. McNulty
Circuit Judge

True Copy

Copies furnished to:

Karen A. Barnett
William Rutger
William Bennett

No. 85-11481
sion 15

R NO. 390674

sent the Sarasota Straightlings to the St. Petersburg branch, which was also under investigation.

Straight's executive director spoke to the *Sarasota Herald-Tribune* about these investigations, saying, "It seems…that no matter how much we do or how much we cooperate, we cannot resolve the issues to their satisfaction."[8] The *St. Petersburg Times* reported that Straight had spent more than $200,000 in lawyers' fees to defend itself, and that the publicity from the investigations and lawsuits had "driven away new clients, forcing new enrollments to drop 40 percent below projections."[9]

Straight's death spiral was slow but well publicized as big media picked up the story. In 1985, the year I entered the program, the American Civil Liberties Union filed a $500,000 lawsuit on behalf of a teen who was put on a diet of only peanut butter and water for nearly a month. As punishment for her refusal to cooperate, she'd been forced to walk naked in front of her host dad.

Florida state prosecutor David Levin, for ABC's *20/20*, described the program as "…a sort of private jail, utilizing techniques such as torture and punishment, which even a convicted criminal would not be subject to."[10]

---

8. Mark Zaloudek, "Straight Suspends Local Drug Program," *Sarasota Herald-Tribune*, July 20, 1983.
9. Milo Geyelin, "State Tells Straight to Change Its Ways," *St. Petersburg Times*, June 21, 1983.
10. Tim O'Brien, "Closure for a Quack Victim," *New Jersey Law Journal*, January 24, 2000.

CBS's *60 Minutes* featured a former host dad, describing Straight's reaction to his concerns about locking kids into rooms at night: "If your child was on the street, the child would die. In the case of a fire, the child would die. So you're not any worse off."[11]

Straight, Inc. reported to have 50,000 clients pass through their warehouses across nine states: California, Florida, Georgia, Maryland, Massachusetts, Michigan, Ohio, Texas, and Virginia.[12] For seventeen years, Straight dominated the adolescent drug treatment industry. But in the end, there were too many investigations, too many lawsuits.

In 1990, it was discovered that Straight was admitting children who had never used drugs. When the state of Massachusetts investigated the Straight, Inc. Boston branch (where I spent the second half of my program), they discovered a twelve-year-old client whose file reported not that she had smoked weed once or twice, that she had never drunk beer...but that she had once sniffed a magic marker.[13]

Game over. The last program called Straight, Inc. closed its doors in 1993.

But that doesn't mean that Straight died. The DNA kept spiraling. Just like Synanon became the Seed became Straight,

---

11. Ed Bradley, "Straight, Inc.," *60 Minutes*, January 29, 1984.
12. Maia Szalavitz, "The Ambassador's Penis Pump and the Damage Done," *The Huffington Post*, May 25, 2011.
13. Michael Langan, "In Mechanics and Mentality the Physician Health Program 'Blueprint' Is Essentially Straight, Inc. for Doctors," *Disrupted Physician*, May 15, 2015.

Straight became new programs, some of which exist to this day. The *Orlando Weekly* described how this process worked: "Straight Orlando shut its doors on August 14, 1992… But it reopened for business the same day, in the same facility, with the same administration. The only real difference was the name: SAFE."[14]

Then there were the copycat programs opened by former Straight parents and staff, such as Miller Newton's KIDS. Virtually identical to Straight, KIDS was able to operate until 1998, despite shelling out millions in lawsuits. One fourteen-year-old girl who had never drunk or used drugs was kept there for six years. She sued and won $4.5 million. A thirteen-year-old with "learning problems" was put into KIDS for wearing a leather skirt, and kept there for thirteen years. She sued and won $6.5 million.[15]

Pathway Family Center, another Straight clone created by Straight parents, operated all the way up through 2009. And Straight-descendent AARC—or Alberta Adolescent Recovery Centre, originally called KIDS of the Alberta Rockies—is still in business today.

While a renamed Straight lives on in Canada, equally destructive programs are operating all over the United States. In 2007, the U.S. government released a report on the

---

14. Jeffrey C. Billman, "SAFE (or else)," *Orlando Weekly*, January 16, 2003.
15. Tim O'Brien, "Keeping 'Cult' Out of the Case," *New Jersey Law Journal*, July 7, 2003.

"troubled teen industry." The report states that, between 34 states, there were 1,503 reports of abuse or neglect of children by residential program staff. Twenty-eight states reported one or more youth fatalities. The report went on to say that these statistics "understate the incidents of maltreatment and death."[16] Program kids are good at keeping their mouths shut.

So now, the big question: how does this happen? The answer is simple: power, greed, and desperation.

Let's start with power. Straight was under investigation, losing lawsuits, yet was able to keep its license to operate. How? A *Tampa Tribune* article headline provides a tidy answer: "Straight chief twisted arms, report shows—politically connected Mel Sembler had help from state senators to get a license renewed."[17] A longtime Republican fund-raiser, Sembler would end up breaking records during George W. Bush's 2000 presidential candidacy: he raised $21.3 million at a single dinner.[18] Today, in addition to fund-raising, he and his wife run the Drug Free America Foundation.

And now, let's move to greed. As Sembler's history illustrates, power + greed = $. Proof: the first of sixteen checks my mother wrote to Straight, Inc. in the 1980s.

---

16. Education and the Workforce, "House Education Committee Approves Legislation to Stop Child Abuse in Teen Residential Programs," February 11, 2009.
17. Annmarie Sarsfield, "Straight Chief Twisted Arms, Report Shows—Politically Connected Mel Sembler Had Help from State Senators to Get a License Renewed," *Tampa Tribune*, July 8, 1993.
18. John Gorenfeld, "Ambassador de Sade," Alternet, November 7, 2005.

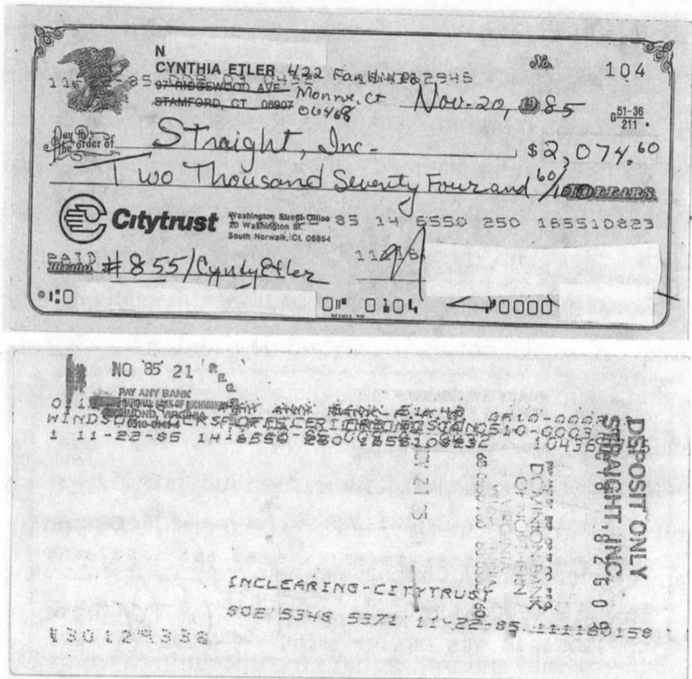
N
CYNTHIA ETLER 422 Farm Hill Rd
Monroe, CT 06468
No. 104
Nov-20, 1985
51-36 / 211
Pay to the order of Straight, Inc. $2,074.60
Two Thousand Seventy Four and 60/100 DOLLARS
Citytrust
Washington Street Office
20 Washington St.
South Norwalk, Ct. 06854
Memo #855/Cyndy Etler

NO '85 21
PAY ANY BANK
DEPOSIT ONLY
STRAIGHT, INC.
INCLEARING-CITYTRUST
11-22-85

This formula still works in today's "troubled teen industry." The "Kids for Cash" scandal is a perfect example. In 2015, a Pennsylvania judge was accused of accepting $1 million in bribes from the owner of a for-profit juvenile jail in exchange for sentencing kids with minor offenses—shoplifting a DVD, making fun of a principal on social media—to extended sentences in the donor's facility. The judge was sentenced to twenty-eight years in prison.[19]

Now, finally, desperation. When teens act rebellious,

19. M. David, "Judge Sentenced to 28 Years for Selling 'Kids for Cash' to Prisons," Counter Current News, August 27, 2015.

parents get scared. When parents don't see options for help, they get desperate. When powerful organizations put out persuasive marketing materials and media directed at desperate parents, those parents buy in.

A writer for *American Conservative* described Straight's best magic trick: "the creation of an image of the lying and manipulating teen which [could] then be applied indiscriminately to all complaints."[20] In other words, Straight convinced parents that their teen—that every teen—was, in fact, a lying druggie scumbag. And once parents wrote that first check—once they were committed—they had to recruit other parents.

A congressional report compared Straight's strategies to Communist brainwashing. When reviewing the comments that committed Straight parents made to the media, there is clear proof of that brainwashing. "I don't know how humane I would've been with my daughters if I didn't have Straight," one dad had said. "I was ready to get violent with them myself."[21]

Regarding the investigation that closed down the Sarasota Straight, one parent (who was also president of the Sarasota Straight's local administrative board) said, "We've got people coming here from states all over, and

20. Eve Tushnet, "We Had to Torture the Children in Order to Save Them," *American Conservative*, October 4, 2012.
21. Mark Zaloudek, "Straight, Inc. Under Fire from Parents," *Sarasota Herald-Tribune*, May 1, 1983.

Parents,

I have noticed while sitting in on some of your pre-intakes that you are getting away from our main purpose. That is, we want these pre-intakes to return for an assessment (remember now?). The Intake parents and Straight Staff will answer all questions regarding the workings of the program and the commitment to same later. DON'T SCARE THEM AWAY!!!!!

It is important to get these parents to talk about themselves and the fact that they may have a drug problem in their home. We are here to offer a service to them, The Assessment !!! Their participatin & commitment to the program comes later after their child has been assessed as being Chemically Dependent. Talk less about your own children, but encourage these parents to realize for themselves that an assessment would be of help.

Remember, when these parents come here, we will put no hurdles, stumbling or road blocks.

NO NOs!!!

Time involved
Hours
Newcomers
Changes in parents
Travel
Fund raising
Volunteering
Restraints
Siblings
Relatives,

ETC

they're desperate. Unless you're in a similar situation, you can't understand [the program's value]...but when you've got government interfering with things they're not knowledgeable about, it's a travesty."[22]

Government is still interfering today, trying to enact laws that protect institutionalized children. In 2008, a bill called H.R. 6358: Stop Child Abuse in Residential Programs for Teens Act of 2008 was introduced. It died in Congress.

In 2009, bill H.R. 911: Stop Child Abuse in Residential Programs for Teens Act of 2009 was introduced. It died in Congress.

In 2015, bipartisan bill H.R. 3060: Stop Child Abuse in Residential Programs for Teens Act of 2015 was introduced, this time by a Democratic congressman and a Republican congresswoman working together. The bill is supported by sixty outside groups, campaigns, and program-survivor networks. Its title reads: "To require certain standards and enforcement provisions to prevent child abuse and neglect in residential programs."

As of this book's publication, the bill is currently awaiting consideration by a congressional committee. According to govtrack.us, a website that tracks the activities of the U.S. Congress, the bill has a 2 percent chance of success.

Because power + greed = $.

---

22. Mark Zaloudek, "Drug Treatment Center Suspends Area Operation," *Sarasota Herald-Tribune*, July 20, 1983.

ACKNOWLEDGMENTS

I feel like the luckiest girl alive, both because I'm still here—a point which was in question when I was a teen—and because I'm *here*, publishing this book. I have so many to thank for helping me get here. And *here*.

The writers: Ellen Hopkins, who opened the door. Russell Banks, who turned on the lights. LouAnne Johnson, who welcomed me into the club, and Dave Eggers, who gave out party favors. Prince, who brought the soul, and Pink Floyd, who brought the oxygen. And Beverly Clearly, James Baldwin, James Frey, Francine Pascal, Jenni Fagan, Maya Angelou, S. E. Hinton, Walter Dean Myers, Judy Blume, Tana French, Walter Mosley, and Zora Neale Hurston, who gave me a place to stay.

The readers: all the students who read and critiqued and demanded more pages from my early drafts. Rachael Wilbur,

Lori Drohan, Dr. Nancy Noonan, Rosella LaFevre, Amanda Dunn, and Judy Storey, who read and (mostly) cheered. The many, many people who wrote to thank me, who wrote reviews, and the two people who wrote to say the book sucked, who made me work harder to ensure that it didn't.

The comrades: the whole Straight survivors' community—who get it automatically—and Kris Flannery, Marcus Chatfield, Ginger McNulty, Kelly Matthews, Maia Szalavitz, Rich Mullinax, and Philip Elberg Esq., the fucking heroes.

The places: Bridgeport, Connecticut; Portland, Oregon; and UMass Boston—for loving and healing and raising me.

The rock stars: Mercy Pilkington, Dr. Rachel Rubin, and Dr. Laura Skinner, who know what they did. And do.

The extended family: Aunt Jane and Uncle George, who saw the writer in me from day one, and all of my high school kids, from Dorchester to Rogers to Vance to MI-WAYE to Turning Point to Hough to Pressly, who better not fucking change.

The book *brujas*: my agent, Myrsini Stephanides, the first to hear the music in the words and to see what I hope I am; who erased every bad day ever with a single email. And to my editorial team at Sourcebooks, especially to Annette Pollert-Morgan, whose superpowers include finding every invisible spot where I tried and tried and went **shrug* good enough*...and sweetly, gently asking the questions that brought it up to *great*.

The random adults: Donna and Bob Santos, Irish Mike,

and the men and women of Trumbull AA, for providing a safe place. And Penny Odell and the Janus House staff, for the care, for the *respect*, and for showing me my destiny.

And my family, my heart, my quad: Eric, Eli, and Oscar, for giving me everything I never thought I could have: peace, safety, and true, simple love.

And maybe most of all, the many of us who couldn't survive the cult. I get it. I'm sorry. And I hope you've found peace and love, too.

ABOUT THE AUTHOR

A modern-day Cinderella, Cyndy Etler was homeless at fourteen and *summa cum laude* at thirty. As a teacher and teen life coach, she convinces kids that books work better than drugs. She lives with her brilliant husband and adorable rescue dogs in North Carolina. Find her at cyndyetler.com.